Matthew W. Herron

The
FAITHFUL
PREACHER

FOREWORD BY JOHN PIPER

The
FAITHFUL
PREACHER

Recapturing the Vision of Three Pioneering
African-American Pastors

THABITI M. ANYABWILE

CROSSWAY BOOKS

A PUBLISHING MINISTRY OF
GOOD NEWS PUBLISHERS
WHEATON, ILLINOIS

The Faithful Preacher

Copyright © 2007 by Thabiti M. Anyabwile

Published by Crossway Books
a publishing ministry of Good News Publishers
1300 Crescent Street
Wheaton, Illinois 60187

Cover design: Jessica Dennis

Cover illustration: Jessica Dennis

First printing, 2007

Printed in the United States of America

Bible quotations are taken from the King James Version.

Library of Congress Cataloging-in-Publication Data
Anyabwile, Thabiti M., 1970–
    The faithful preacher : recapturing the vision of three pioneering
African-American pastors / Thabiti M. Anyabwile.
        p. cm.
    ISBN 13: 978-1-58134-827-9 (tpb)
    ISBN 10: 1-58134-827-4
    1. African Americans—Religion. 2. African American clergy.
3. Pastoral theology. 4. Haynes, Lemuel, 1753–1833. 5. Payne, Daniel
Alexander, 1811–1893. 6. Grimké, Francis J. (Francis James), 1850–1937.
I. Title.
BR563.N4A59   2007
277.3'08092396073—dc22   2006017146

MLY		17	16	15	14	13	12	11	10	09	08	07
15	14	13	12	11	10	9	8	7	6	5	4	3	2	1

Above all . . .
for the glory of Christ Jesus the Savior.

With thanks to the Father for Kristie, my wife,
the tangible expression of the Father's favor to me.
(Proverbs 18:22)

With thanks to God for Afiya and Eden, my daughters,
who lovingly asked, "Daddy, how's the book coming?"
and spurred me on to completion.

To my God and my Savior,
my wife, and my daughters . . . with love.

CONTENTS

FOREWORD

By John Piper

I have been happily drawn into this book because it embodies four passions of my life. First, it is rooted in the big biblical vision of the sovereign God called reformed theology. Second, it expresses the wise conviction that knowing history and biography will protect us from trendiness in the ministry and will reveal the blind spots of our own age and enrich us with the insights that other generations have received. Third, it mines the unknown riches of the African-American experience and lays hold on the truth that their suffering was not in vain but has treasures for our time not yet dreamed of. Fourth, it lifts us above the low, managerial, psychologized, pragmatic, organizational view of the pastoral office and sets us in the high, clean air and bright light of the biblical vision of what it means to be called to shepherd the blood-bought bride of Christ.

You are about to meet three African-American pastors—Lemuel Haynes (1753–1833), Daniel A. Payne (1811–1893), and Francis Grimké (1850–1937). Their pastoral and educational ministries total over 130 years of faithfulness to God's people. You will be introduced to them biographically by the able hand of Thabiti Anyabwile. Then you will meet them in their own words. This book is mainly to be prized as the never-before-gathered collection of African-American writings on the pastoral ministry from a time that spans 150 years and stretches across the terrible Civil War of our nation.

In this book we who are not African-American receive the double profit of reading not only across a culture but across the centuries—and thus across another culture. And, of course, that implies that the African-American reader will read across another culture as well. My guess and my prayer is that these unusual crossings will weave our lives and ministries together in ways we have not foreseen.

There are surprises ahead. Did you know there was such a thing as

9

"black puritans"? The author describes all three of these brothers like this: "They were puritans. They committed themselves to sound theology in the pulpit, theologically informed practice in the church, and theologically reformed living in the world."

Did you know that, in the words of John Saillant, "From Calvinism, this generation of black authors (referring specifically to Lemuel Haynes) drew a vision of God at work providentially in the lives of black people, directing their sufferings yet promising the faithful among them a restoration to his favor and his presence"?

Did you know that in 1835 the South Carolina Assembly passed a law that said, "[If] any free person of color or slave shall keep any school or other place of instruction for teaching any slave or free person of color to read or write, such free person of color or slave shall be liable to the same fine, imprisonment, and corporal punishment as are by this Act imposed and afflicted upon free persons of color and slaves for teaching slaves to read or write"? This forced the closing of Daniel Payne's school and led him to work out his vision for an educated black ministry within the northern context of the African Methodist Episcopal Church and in the leadership of Wilberforce University in Ohio, "the first institution of higher education owned and operated by African-Americans."

Did you know that it was even possible for a free black man (Lemuel Haynes) in the eighteenth century to marry a white woman and pastor an all-white congregation in Vermont for over thirty years?

Did you know that Charles Hodge, professor of theology at Princeton Seminary, taught African-American students such as Francis Grimké, who took the great reformed vision of God and spent his life working out its implications for race relations in the church while serving as pastor of 15th Street Presbyterian Church in Washington, D.C.?

So there will be surprises. But what should be no surprise is that there are treasures of biblical wisdom in centuries before our own and in cultures not our own. I love the blow this book makes against chronological snobbery and ethnocentricity. May the Lord of the Church, for the good of His people and the ingathering of His lost sheep and the glory of His name, give this book good success.

John Piper
Pastor for Preaching and Vision,
Bethlehem Baptist Church, Minneapolis

ACKNOWLEDGMENTS

God, in His kindness, allows some men and women to set ideas into print and to see those ideas published for others. Such an opportunity is a great blessing. And that blessing is accompanied by other blessings in the form of loved ones, family and friends, and critics who support your efforts and make it better. This acknowledgments page is an acknowledgment of both blessings from God.

To God alone belongs any praise for any edification that this volume offers the reading world. To God alone belongs the praise for the fruitfulness of the men and ministries featured here. To God alone belongs the praise for providentially ordering my reading life so that I would be introduced to these men and find opportunity to assemble a sampling of their work. I acknowledge God in all these things and more; to Him belongs the glory.

I thank God always when I remember my wife, Kristie, who without fail is my biggest encourager and cheerleader. She has ever had my back in life and ministry. Sweetie, "I see you in my eyes."

I thank God too for Afiya and Eden, my daughters. It's an indescribable pleasure to have your six- and four-year-old daughters interested in your ministry. Thank you, girls, for all the times you stopped by my desk with snacks and presents and to ask, "Daddy, how's your book coming?" I pray and trust there are crowns in heaven for you for your tender example of love and service.

God blessed me with two friends who helped make this work possible—Mark Dever and C. J. Mahaney. Brothers, I have learned so much from you, and I pray that the Lord will multiply all our labors for His glory. Thank you for your tireless example of faithful pastoral ministry. You brothers are rock-solid friends and mentors, and I praise God for placing you in my life.

Acknowledgments

I also praise God for the blessing of John Piper, who authored the foreword to this volume and through whom the Lord has been pleased to teach this generation to exult in the excellencies of Jesus Christ.

And then there is the gift of God's church. At the writing of this book, I was a member, elder, and assistant pastor at Capitol Hill Baptist Church. I praise God for CHBC whose love, encouragements, prayer, and joy redound to God's glory and to my blessing. I want to especially thank Cathy Boehme, John Keim, Sam Lam, Gio Lynch, and John and Dawn Ingold for their faithful comments and their editing of this volume. May your labors bear much fruit.

I also praise the Lord for the faithfulness of the family at Crossway Books, who care more about the truth of God than the ring of sales.

To God be the glory!

INTRODUCTION

As I complete this book, I am at the eve of a dream come true—serving the Lord in full-time Christian ministry as a senior pastor. Over the past several years I have served as an elder in two churches, helped plant one of those churches, and carried on an itinerant preaching and evangelism ministry. Over the years and throughout these ministry opportunities, my desire for serving in pastoral ministry, for shepherding the people of His pasture, has steadily grown and has at times been nearly overwhelming.

However, sitting on the eve of that dream, I am stalked by questions and uncertainties that at some point surely haunt every man in the ministry. In fact, it is in some measure the uncertainties and the questions that prepare a man for the ministry—they keep him humble and dependent upon the Lord for wisdom and guidance. So I have come to embrace my questions as a particular form of grace from God. Still, questions and uncertainties call for answers and resolve.

Many questions depend largely on individual circumstances—whether the person involved is married or single, whether he has children, how much experience he has, whether he is educated for the task, gifted, sure of his calling, etc. However, most questions fall generally into one of three categories:
- What does the Lord require of His pastors?
- How must I prepare for this calling, and am I ready?
- What is the pastor's responsibility outside the church, for engaging the world?

Bookshelves in Christian bookstores are filled with answers to these and other questions involving pastoral ministry. Some of them are classics and well worth reading. Others promise great payoffs for little effort and "new ideas for today's ministry." The array of options is dizzying. Yet most of these new ideas have one fatal flaw in common—because they are new, they are not proven. These proposals on how to build an effective church or become a successful pastor generally lack any track record beyond the personal experiences of the individual authors. So the honest reader faces the daunting task of evaluating the worthiness of these various perspectives, gauging, usually through trial and error, whether the approaches will work in their local churches and whether their effects are good or bad, faithful or unfaithful to biblical truth. But who really wants to approach shepherding the Lord's sheep by trial and error?

As I have prepared for my own journey into ministry, wading through a truckload of trees used to print hundreds of books aimed at pastors, my experience confirmed that old folk wisdom, "all that glitters is not gold"—especially when it is extolled as a new form of gold. As I have sought for a better way, a better understanding, and a biblically faithful perspective, it has pleased my soul to realize that the old ideas are still the best ideas. Those who have gone before us, old friends with old ideas, have left us a proven track record of faithfulness and fruitfulness. And the two do go together: where there is faithfulness, fruitfulness is bound to follow.

We are told from the time we are schoolchildren that "those who do not learn from history are doomed to repeat it." Maintaining an ignorance of history will not result in the replication of greatness and earlier success. Those who learn from history, who wisely consult those who have gone before, are the only ones who have a real chance at succeeding and avoiding pitfalls. Faithfulness and fruitfulness in ministry require wisdom, hard work, time, and the providential blessings of God, all of which are enhanced by a humble study of our predecessors.

The best place to learn and prepare for the ministry is still at the feet of the Master Himself, and from His apostles. Who would not want to study under Paul or Peter? To hear their account of firsthand experiences with our Lord? Jesus, Paul, Peter, and others are still available to us, to speak with us through God's Word. And I trust that every faithful pastor is learning, studying, praying, and seeking wisdom and grace for the task from them.

But also available to us are "lesser" luminaries, men who were not apostles but who were faithful students and shepherds. Christian history is filled with Spurgeons, Calvins, Luthers, and others who have had to answer tough questions, face uncertainties, and persevere in faith as they led God's people. From them the wise pastor gains valuable insights and observes patterns of godliness for his own ministry.

This book profiles three "lesser" luminaries from the African-American experience—Lemuel Haynes, Bishop Daniel Alexander Payne, and Dr. Francis Grimké. They are "lesser" luminaries in the sense that they are not worthy of comparison to the Lord and in the sense that the Lord's apostles had unique ministries in Christian history. But they are not lesser to other saints in their passion for God, in their love for God's people, in their zeal for a pure church, or in the wisdom they leave behind for pastors and leaders of the church.

In Haynes, Payne, and Grimké you will find great models of and exhortations to faithfulness. Lemuel Haynes, a former indentured servant, served as pastor of an all-white congregational church for thirty-three years in Rutland, Vermont—an unheard of feat for an African-American of his period and ours. Bishop Payne served over forty years as pastor, bishop, and university president. Dr. Grimké gave nearly six decades of his life to serving as pastor of 15th Street Presbyterian Church in Washington, D.C. These men were faithful to their Lord, their calling, and the people in their charge.

Related to their faithfulness is their longevity. Their careers span most major periods in American history, including the American Revolution, slavery at the height of its power, the Civil War, Emancipation and Reconstruction, and World War I. Through these periods, they faced extreme hardships. None of them were born into privilege. All of them either witnessed or tasted the lash of slavery and the racial prejudices that followed that institution. Around them American society changed radically. However, their commitment to the ministry and their understanding of it remained constant. They continued in the same glorious work of proclaiming the gospel "instant in season, out of season" (2 Timothy 4:2).

But principally these men are included here for their consistently high and biblical view of the pastoral ministry. They greatly esteemed the privilege and responsibility of caring for God's people, of cultivating and leading a "pure" church, and of dedicating one's self to representing Christ before a dying world. They were puritans. They committed themselves to sound theology in the pulpit, theologically informed practice in the church, and theologically reformed living in the world. They saw

Christ in all things and endeavored to see Him glorified before all people. They were from the African-American tradition of Christianity, but like all true saints, they belong to all Christians of every background and era. They were gifts to the Body of Christ from Christ Himself, and they will befriend every leader with a God-given desire to glorify Christ through beautifying the church.

Lemuel Haynes reminds us to view the pastoral ministry from the vantage point of eternity and the accounting that pastors will give to the Lord of the Church. Daniel Alexander Payne instructs us on how preparation and education, both in intellect and character, affect the minister and the people in his charge. And Francis Grimké challenges us to remember that the church and the pastor, as they confront the world and its problems, are first and foremost to preach the gospel and to live the gospel.

For many readers, this volume will be an introduction to these men and their careers. For others, Haynes, Payne, and Grimké are already old friends. Both the newcomer and the longtime acquaintance will be rewarded for reading these pastors and will find answers for many of the questions and concerns that face us today. These are representatives of the old ideas that have served and preserved the church for over two thousand years.

PART ONE

Lemuel Haynes:

Pastoral Ministry in Light of Eternity

If the church is to prosper and mature, she will need faithful men to lead and care for her. The church will need men who are sound in doctrine, whose lives are guided by the Word of God, and who are willing to defend the truth. The church will need to hold up as its ideal those who model fidelity and love toward God, men who will pour themselves out for the benefit of the Lord's sheep. Men of this mold are gifts to the church from her Lord. In the late 1700s the Lord did indeed give such a gift to the church—Lemuel Haynes.

Lemuel Haynes was born on July 18, 1753 in West Hartford, Connecticut. Early biographers speculated that Haynes's mother was either a daughter of the prominent Goodwin family of Hartford or a servant named Alice Fitch who worked for one John Haynes. However, speculations about his parentage proved profitless. Abandoned by his parents at five months of age, Haynes was raised as an indentured servant by the Rose family in Middle Granville, Massachusetts. The Roses treated Lemuel as one of the family's own children, giving him the same pious instruction in Christianity and family worship that Deacon Rose gave all his children.[1]

Following his indenture, Haynes volunteered in 1774 as a Minuteman and in October 1776 joined the Continental Army, thus becoming part of the American Revolution. Haynes volunteered just as the Continental

Navy and Army suffered heavy casualties at the Battle of Valcour Bay on October 11, 1776 and General Washington's forces met defeat at the Battle of White Plains on October 28, 1776. In November 1776 Continental forces witnessed over three thousand casualties and the loss of over one hundred cannons and thousands of muskets in defeats at Fort Washington and Fort Lee. Lemuel served in the Continental Army until November 17, 1776, when he contracted typhus and was relieved of duty. Despite the dismal prospects of the Revolution at this point, as a patriot Haynes was determined to defend with life and tongue the newly developing nation and its ideals of liberty. His political values were shaped by his "idealization of George Washington and allegiance to the Federalist Party."[2]

But it was during his time with the Rose family and after the American Revolution that Haynes demonstrated his interests and talents for theology and ministry. "Haynes was a determined, self-taught student who pored over Scripture until he could repeat from memory most of the texts dealing with the doctrines of grace."[3] Though Haynes benefited from the devout religious practice and instruction of Deacon Rose, the works of Jonathan Edwards, George Whitefield, and Philip Doddridge influenced him the most. Indeed, Haynes owed much to the revival and evangelism efforts of Whitefield and Edwards, who greatly impacted America, and especially the New England area, during the Great Awakening of the 1740s.

Haynes began his formal ministerial training by studying Greek and Latin with two Connecticut clergymen, Daniel Farrand and William Bradford. He was licensed to preach on November 29, 1780 and five years later became the first African-American ordained by any religious body in America. In 1804 Middlebury College awarded Haynes an honorary Master's degree—another first for an African-American.

Owing largely to his Puritan-like experiences with the Rose family and his admiration of Whitefield and Edwards, Haynes adopted a decidedly Calvinistic theology. Calvinism was typical of African-American writers during Haynes's lifetime. One biographer, reflecting on a host of African-American writers in the late 1700s, observed:

> Indeed, Calvinism seems to have corroborated the deepest structuring elements of the experiences of such men and women as they matured

from children living in slavery or servitude into adults desiring freedom, literacy, and membership in a fair society. From Calvinism, this generation of black authors drew a vision of God at work providentially in the lives of black people, directing their sufferings yet promising the faithful among them a restoration to his favor and his presence. Not until around 1815 would African American authors, such as John Jea, explicitly declare themselves against Calvinism and for free-will religion.[4]

Despite what appeared to be a Calvinistic hegemony, the New England area was not without its disputes and controversies. Following the First Great Awakening, significant arguments regarding church membership, salvation, assurance, and the revivals themselves unsettled and divided churches. Jonathan Edwards, one of Haynes's theological influences, was fired from his Northampton pastorate for refusing to administer Communion to church members and their children who, though morally upstanding, did not profess saving faith in Christ, a practice known as the "half-way covenant." Other churches divided into "New Light," "Old Light," and "Moderate" local assemblies. New Light congregations welcomed the revival of the Great Awakening with open arms, while their Old Light counterparts opposed the revival and the emotional excesses that accompanied it. Moderates attempted a middle-of-the-road understanding that recognized God's activity in the revival but sought to curb emotionalism. These ecclesial and theological controversies were the protean matter of Haynes's intellectual formation. Haynes was a "New Light moderate" and a strict Congregationalist who favored the independence of the local church and the need for a regenerate membership.

Lemuel Haynes's pastoral career spanned forty years. He began his life of Christian service as a founding member and supply pastor to the church in Middle Granville, Massachusetts. He served in Middle Granville for five years, then received ordination from the Association of Ministers in Litchfield County, Connecticut. Haynes completed his ordination in 1785 while serving a church in Torrington, Connecticut. However, despite his evident prowess as a preacher, he was never offered the pastorate of that church due to racial prejudice and resentment among some churches in the area. In 1783 Haynes met and married twenty-year-old Elizabeth Babbit, a young white schoolteacher and a member of the Middle Granville congregation. The couple bore ten children between 1785 and 1805.

On March 28, 1788 Haynes left the Torrington congregation and accepted a call to pastor the west parish of Rutland, Vermont, where he served the all-white congregation for thirty years—a relationship between pastor and congregation rare in Haynes's time and in ours both for its length and for its racial dynamic. During his stay in Rutland, the church grew in membership from forty-two congregants to about three hundred and fifty as Haynes modeled pastoral devotedness and fidelity to the people in his charge. He also emerged as a defender of Calvinistic orthodoxy, opposing the encroachment of Arminianism, universalism, and other errors.

In March 1818, on the heels of a five-year-long dispute with a deacon and growing alienation between Haynes and members of the congregation, several of whom were facing various church discipline charges, the church voted against continuing its relationship with their pastor of thirty years. In his farewell sermon to the Rutland congregation, "The Sufferings, Support, and Reward of Faithful Ministers, Illustrated," Lemuel Haynes concluded:

> The flower of my life has been devoted to your service:—and while I lament a thousand imperfections which have attended my ministry; yet if I am not deceived, it has been my hearty desire to do something for the salvation of your souls.

Following his tenure in Rutland, Haynes remained active in ministry, serving despite declining health. He served as pastor in Manchester, Vermont from 1818 until 1822. In 1822 he began an eleven-year preaching ministry with a church in Granville, New York. Haynes contracted a gangrenous infection in one of his feet in March 1833. But he continued his duties with the Granville, New York congregation until May of that year, when health limitations overtook him. Lemuel Haynes died on September 28, 1833 at the age of eighty.[5]

As a pastor, Haynes seemed always to be possessed with thoughts of the welfare of his congregation. Their salvation was paramount. His sermons made explicit the centrality of the cross of Christ and were rich in both theological instruction and practical application for his hearers. Lemuel Haynes is a wonderful model of the "old ideas" that stand the test of time and point the way forward even in our day.

The sermons included in this volume provide a glimpse into Haynes's understanding of pastoral ministry. In general, an eschatological expectation gripped Haynes's heart and mind. In each of the selections included here, the anticipation of meeting the Lord Jesus Christ at the Judgment motivated Haynes's instructions to his hearers. Haynes well understood that the bar of Christ, especially for the minister, would be a time of penetrating judgment, a time at which the heart and habits of the pastor would be laid bare and his just rewards made known.

Consequently, Haynes believed that a minister's Christian character was essential to his faithfulness and to his effectiveness in the gospel ministry. In a 1792 ordination sermon, "The Character and Work of a Spiritual Watchman Described," Haynes underscored five key traits a minister needs to possess. First, they are to "love the cause in which they profess to embark." That is, they must love Christ Himself and the proclamation of His divine glory to those who would hear and be saved. Second, the minister is to be wise and prudent, understanding the subtlety of the spiritual task and the spiritual enemies against whom he is engaged. Third, patience must accompany every member of the ministry. Fourth, courage and fortitude must fill his heart. And fifth, vigilance, alertness, and close attention to the business of watching for souls must characterize the spiritual watchman, the faithful preacher. Apart from these qualifications, the Christian minister is completely unprepared to give an account to God for his conduct and his care for God's people. But those who are prepared would examine their motives for entering the ministry, would be careful to know their duties as pastors, would seek to please none but God, would work to make their preaching plain, sober, modest, and reverent, and would work to know as much as possible about the souls entrusted to their care.

Haynes's eschatological vision of pastoral ministry was displayed most clearly in a 1798 funeral sermon entitled "The Important Concerns of Ministers and the People of Their Charge." In this sermon Haynes anticipated that the pastor and the congregation would have a special relationship to one another in the coming judgment of Christ, where the congregation would be the "hope, or joy, or crown of rejoicing . . . in the presence of our Lord Jesus Christ at his coming."[6] However, the Second Coming of Christ and the accompanying judgment of ministers and their people was, in Haynes's estimation, a proposition filled with both joyous promise and striking terror. At stake, more than merely the souls of pastors and congregants, was the very glory of God Himself—whether the character of the Redeemer was properly displayed before His creation through the ministry of which both minister and member were a part. If the pastor was faithful, the congregation and their shepherd would enjoy a special intimacy with one another, an intimacy deepened by the congregants' commendation of the pastor and by the pastor's recommendation of his people before the Lord Himself. However, if either the pastor or the congregation were unfaithful, their eternal relationship would be one of accusing and exposing the other before God and His Son. For everlasting good or for eternal ill, the pastor and the congregation were joined in a most solemn union before God, according to Haynes. Haynes concluded, "The influence of a faithful or unfaithful minister is such as to effect unborn ages; it will commonly determine the sentiments and characters of their successors, and in this way they may be doing good or evil after they are dead, and even to the second coming of Christ." The unfaithful minister would be tried for his treasonous neglect of the souls of the people, and the unfaithful congregation would stand to hear the pastor's denouncement of their spiritual apathy and hardheartedness. Therefore, ministers ought to preach, and people ought to listen, "with death and judgment in view."

After three decades of pastoral ministry, the church in Rutland, Vermont discharged Lemuel Haynes from his pulpit. By most accounts, the strong sin of racial prejudice finally overcame some members of the congregation who challenged Haynes's leadership. At the occasion of his farewell sermon, "The Sufferings, Support, and Reward of Faithful Ministers, Illustrated," Haynes only briefly recounted some of his thirty years in Rutland. For the most part he took the opportunity to instruct the congregation one last time in the calling, character, and challenges of pastoral ministry. Perhaps feeling the sting of his own situation, Haynes focused on the joys and sorrows that accompany faithfulness in ministers. Faithful ministers are commissioned and sent by Christ as His ambassadors and messengers, a commission that determines their direction and manner in ministry, including how and what to preach and how long they are to serve in a particular place. That commission, asserted Haynes, sometimes ends quickly for the faithful minister:

> The lives of ministers are often shortened by the trials they meet with;
> some times they are actually put to death for the sake of the gospel: they

can say with this holy apostle, As dying, and behold we live! As chastened, and not killed; As sorrowing, yet always rejoicing. The memory of a Patrick, a Beveridge, a Manton, a Flavel, a Watts, a Doddridge, an Edwards, Hopkins, Bellamy, Spencer and Fuller is previous to us; but alas! we see them no more. No more in their studies; no more the visitants of their bereaved flock; no more in their chapels or sanctuaries on earth. They have run their race, finished their course, and are receiving their reward. Their successors in office are pursuing them with rapid speed: and will soon, very soon accomplish their work.

Haynes anticipated that his own demise would follow shortly after leaving the pulpit in Rutland. But for all the bonds and afflictions, briars and thorns, vilification, and opposition faced by faithful ministers, the faithful ministers were never to despair or lose heart because their lot in eternity would be great joy and satisfaction with their Master.

For those in or contemplating entrance into pastoral ministry, Lemuel Haynes reminds us of the solemn importance of faithfulness in the gospel minister. Haynes warns us of a blithe attitude toward our work as ministers, ambassadors for Jesus Christ. Indifference is deadly—to our people and to ourselves. Ours is a life dedicated to caring for another's children with the anticipation of one day returning them to their Heavenly Father. At that time we shall give an account of our stewardship—what we have taught His children, what model or example we have provided, whether we have tended to the state of their souls, and most importantly, whether we spoke reproachfully or gloriously of their True Father. If we would be faithful, we must keep the coming of our Lord in full view as we discharge all the duties we have been given by Him who walks in the midst of the seven lampstands (Revelation 1:13).

Sketch of Rev. Lemuel Haynes, a frontispiece in Timothy Mather Cooley,
Sketches of the Life and Character of the Rev. Lemuel Haynes, A.M.,
for Many Years Pastor of a Church in Rutland, Vt., and Later in Granville,
New York (1837; reprint, New York: Negro Universities Press, 1969).

The Character and Work of a Spiritual Watchman Described (1792)

Haynes's first published sermon was preached at the ordination of Rev. Reuben Parmelee (1759–1843), the first minister of the seven families (nine members) who gathered together to form the First Congregational Church, Hinesburgh, Vermont. The sermon was likely preached in 1791, when the first organized church was established through the efforts of Parmelee. For three years prior Christians had met in homes and farms and in the open air with no consistent pastoral oversight. While most sources assume the sermon was published in 1791, it was probably the first publication of the printing partnership of Collier and Buel of Litchfield, Connecticut, in 1792.

The Character and Work of a Spiritual Watchman Described, a Sermon, Delivered at Hinesburgh, February 23, 1791, at the Ordination of the Rev. Reuben Parmelee

For they watch for your souls, as they that must give account.
— HEBREWS 13:17

Nothing is more evident than that men are prejudiced against the gospel. It is from this source that those who are for the defense of it meet with so much contempt. It is true, they are frail, sinful dust and ashes, in common with other men; yet on account of the important embassy with which they are entrusted, it is agreeable to the unerring dictates of inspiration "to esteem them very highly in love for their work's sake" (1 Thess. 5:13).

To illustrate this sentiment was the delight of the apostle in this verse: "Obey them that have the rule over you, and submit yourselves." He was far from inculcating anything that might seem to confront what the apostle Peter has enjoined in 1 Peter 5:3, "neither as being lords over God's heritage." The word signifies to *lead*, *guide*, or *direct* (Guyse's paraphrase).

25

Our text contains an important motive—to excite the attention and respect that is due to the ministers of Christ on account of their relation to Him. This involves the aspect that their work has to a judgment-day: "For they watch for your souls, as they that must give account." They are amenable to their great Lord and Master for every sermon they preach and must give an account of the reception they and their work met with among their hearers. Under the influence of such a thought, let us take notice of a few things, supposed by the work assigned to ministers in the text, and say something with respect to their character, whence it appears that they must give account when they may be said to be properly influenced by such considerations.

I. There are several ideas suggested by the work assigned to gospel ministers in the text, which is, *to watch for souls.*

This supposes,

1. That the soul is of vast importance; else why so much attention paid to it as to have a guard to inspect it? All those injunctions we find interpreted through the sacred pages to watchmen to be faithful are so many evidences of the worth of men's souls. What renders them so valuable is the important relation they stand in to their Maker. The perfections of the Deity are more illustrated in the redemption of fallen men than they would have been in the salvation of apostate angels; else why were the latter passed by, while God chose the former as the objects of His attention? God has from eternity appointed a proper number for the display of His mercy and justice; means are necessary to fit them for the Master's use; so the soul, in this view, is of infinite importance.

2. Being commanded to be watchmen over the souls of men implies that they are prone to neglect them or to be inattentive to those souls. When one is set to inspect or watch over another, it supposes some kind of incapacity that the individual is under to take care of himself. The Scripture represents mankind by nature as fools, madmen, being in a state of darkness, etc.

Men in general are very sagacious with respect to temporal affairs and display much natural wit and ingenuity in contriving and accomplishing evil designs; "but to do good they have no knowledge" (Jer. 4:22). This is an evidence that their inability to foresee danger and provide against it is of the moral kind. If there were a disposition in mankind, correspondent to their natural powers, to secure the eternal interest of their souls in the way God has proscribed, watchmen would in a great measure be useless.

3. The work and office of gospel ministers suggests the idea of enemies invading, that there is a controversy subsisting, and danger approaching. When soldiers are called forth, and sentinels stand upon the wall, it denotes war. The souls of men are environed with ten thousand enemies that are seeking their ruin. Earth and hell are combined together to destroy. How many already have fallen victims to their ferocity! The infernal powers are daily dragging their prey to the prison of hell. Men have rebelled against God and made him their enemy; yea, all creatures, and all events, are working the eternal misery of the finally impenitent sinner.

4. We are taught in the text and elsewhere that the work of a gospel minister is not with the temporal but with the spiritual concerns of men: they watch for *souls*. Their conversation is not to be about worldly affairs but about things that relate to Christ's kingdom, which involves the everlasting concerns of men's souls. When a minister's affections are upon this world, his visits among his people will be barren. He will inquire about the outward circumstances of his flock and perhaps, from pecuniary motives, rejoice at prosperity, as though that was of greatest concern. But he will have nothing to say with respect to the health and prosperity of their souls, having no joys or sorrows to express on account of the fruitful or lifeless state of the inward man.

II. Let us say something with respect to the character of a spiritual watchman.

Natural endowments, embellished with good education, are qualifications so obviously requisite in an evangelical minister that it is needless for us to insist upon them at this time; and that the interest of religion has, and still continues, greatly to suffer for the want of them is equally notorious.

In the early ages of Christianity, men were miraculously qualified and called into this work of the gospel ministry; but we are far from believing that this is the present mode by which ordinary ministers are introduced.

1. It is necessary that those who engage in this work love the cause in which they profess to be embarked; the love of Christ must be shed abroad in their hearts. Hence our blessed Lord, by whose repeated inter-

rogations to Simon whether he loved Him, has set before us the importance of this qualification in a spiritual shepherd. The sad consequences of admitting those into the army who are in heart enemies to the commonwealth have often taught men to be careful in this particular. The trust reposed in a watchman is such as renders him also capable of great detriment to the community. He that undertakes this work from secular motives will meet with disappointment. What a gross absurdity it is for a man to commend religion to others, while he is a stranger to it himself. "The pious preacher will commend the Savior from the personal fund of his own experience." Being smitten with the love of Christ himself, with what zeal and fervor will he speak of the divine glory! Love to Christ will tend to make a minister faithful and successful. The importance of this point urges me to be copious on the subject, were it not too obvious to require a long discussion.

2. Wisdom and prudence are important qualifications in ministers: hence that injunction of the Great Preacher (Matt. 10:16): "Be ye therefore wise as serpents, and harmless as doves." Such a minister is a man of spiritual understanding whose soul is irradiated with the beams of the Son of Righteousness, has received an unction from the Holy One, is taught by the Word and Spirit, and walks in the light of God's countenance. He has seen the deceit of his own heart, knows the intrigues of the enemy, sees the many snares to which the souls of men are exposed, and, not being ignorant of the devices of Satan, will endeavor to carry on the spiritual campaign with such care and prudence that the enemy shall not get an advantage. He knows that he has a subtle enemy to oppose, and also human nature, replete with enmity against the gospel; and he will endeavor in every effort to conduct himself with that wisdom and circumspection as shall appear most likely to prove successful.

3. Patience is another very necessary qualification in a spiritual watchman. Being inspired with love to the cause, he will stand the storms of temptation and will not be disheartened by all the fatigue and suffering to which his work exposes him but will endure hardness as a good soldier of Jesus Christ.

4. Courage and fortitude must constitute part of the character of a gospel minister. A sentinel who is worthy of that station will not fear the formidable appearance of the enemies, nor tremble at their menaces. None of these things will move him, neither will he count his life dear

unto him as he defends a cause so very important. He has the spirit of intrepid Nehemiah: "Should such a man as I flee?" (6:11). He stands fast in the faith, conducts himself like a man, and is strong.

5. Nor must we forget to mention vigilance, or close attention to the business assigned him, as an essential qualification in a minister of Christ. A man does not answer the idea of a watchman unless his mind is engaged in the business. The word that is rendered "watch" in the text [Heb. 13:17] signifies, in the original, to awake, to abstain from sleeping (Leigh's *Critica Sacra*). Indeed all the purposes of a watchman set upon a wall are frustrated if he sleeps on guard; thereby he himself and the whole army are liable to fall easy prey to the cruel depredations of the enemy. The spiritual watchman is not to sleep but to watch for the first motion of the enemy and give the alarm, lest souls should perish through his drowsiness and inattention.

Some further observations with respect to the work of a gospel minister will be made in their place.

III. We will now show that ministers must give account to God of their conduct, especially as it concerns the people under their charge.

This solemn consideration is suggested in the text below. It is the design of preaching to make things ready for the day of judgment. "To the one we are the savour of death unto death; and to the other the savour of life unto life" (2 Cor. 2:16). We are fitting men for the Master's use, preparing affairs for that decisive court. This supposes that things must be laid open before the great assembly at the day of judgment, or why is it that so many things relate thereto and are preparatives thereof?

The work of a gospel minister has a peculiar relation to the future. An approaching judgment is that to which every subject is pointing and that renders every sentiment to be inculcated vastly solemn and interesting. Ministers are accountable creatures in common with other men; and we have the unerring testimony of Scripture that "God shall bring every work into judgment, with every secret thing, whether it be good, or whether it be evil" (Eccles. 12:14). If none of our conduct is too minute to be known, we may well conclude that important affairs relating to the work and office of gospel ministers will not pass unnoticed.

Arguments taken from the names given to the ministers of Christ show that they must give account. They are called soldiers, ambassadors, servants, stewards, etc., which points out the relation they and their work stand in to God: they are sent by God and are answerable to Him who sent them, just as a servant or steward is to give account to his lord and master with respect to his faithfulness in the trust reposed in him. God tells Ezekiel that if watchmen are not faithful, and souls perish through their neglect, He will require their blood at the hands of such careless watchmen. It is evident that early ministers were influenced to practice faithfulness from a view of the solemn account they expected to give at the day of judgment. This gave rise to those words, "But Peter and John answered and said unto them, Whether it be right in the sight of God to hearken unto you more than unto God, judge ye" (Acts 4:19). If God's omniscience is a motive to be faithful, that must be because of the view that he will not let our conduct pass unnoticed but will call us to an account.

It was approaching judgment that engrossed the attention of Paul and made him exhort Timothy to study to approve himself unto God. This also made the beloved disciple speak of having "boldness in the day of judgment" (1 John 4:17).

The Divine Glory is the only object worthy of attention, and to display His holy character was the design of God in creation, as there were no other beings existing antecedent to attract the mind of Jehovah. And we are sure that God is pursuing the same thing still, and always will. "He is in one mind, and who can turn him?" (Job 23:13). There is no conceivable object that bears any proportion with the glory of God; and for Him ever to aim at anything else would be incompatible with His perfections. The day of judgment is designed to be a comment on all other days; at that time God's government of the world and the conduct of all toward Him will be publicly investigated, that the equity of divine administration may appear conspicuous before the assembled universe. It is called a day "when the Son of man is *revealed*" (Luke 17:30). The honor of God requires that matters be publicly and particularly attended to, that evidences be summoned at this open court. Hence the saints are to judge the world (1 Cor. 6:2).

It will lead to the mutual happiness of faithful ministers and the people to have matters laid open before the bar of God, so that, as in the words following our text, they may do it with joy and not with grief. The apostle speaks of some ministers and people who should have reciprocal joy in the day of the Lord Jesus, which supposes that ministers and the people under their charge are to meet another day as having something special with each other. The connection between ministers and people is such as renders them capable of saying much for or against the people under their charge, with hearers making the same observations in respect to their teachers; and in this way the mercy and justice of God will appear illustrious.

Since, therefore, the work of gospel ministers has such a near relation to a judgment day, since they are accountable creatures and their work so momentous, since this is a sentiment that has had so powerful influence on all true ministers in all ages of the world, the connection is such as to render them capable of saying many things relating to the people under their charge. Above all, since the displays of divine glory are so highly concerned in this matter, we may without hesitation adopt the idea in the text—namely, that ministers will give a solemn account to their great Lord and Master regarding how they discharged the trust reposed in them.

IV. We are to inquire what influence such considerations will have on the true ministers of Christ, or when they may be said to preach and act as those who must give account.

1. Those who properly expect to give account will be very careful to examine themselves with respect to the motives by which they are influenced to undertake this work. Such a minister will view himself as acting in the presence of a heart-searching God who requires truth in the inward part and will shortly call him to account for all the exercises of his heart. He will search every corner of his soul to determine whether the divine honor or something else is the object of his pursuit. He has been taught by the rectitude of the divine law that God will not pass by transgressors but will judge the secrets of men. The work will appear so great that nature will recoil at the thought, like Jeremiah: "Ah, Lord GOD! behold, I cannot speak: for I am a child" (Jer. 1:6). Or with the great apostle, "Who is sufficient for these things?" (2 Cor. 2:16). The true disciple of Jesus will not thrust himself forward into the ministry like a heedless usurper but with the greatest caution and self-diffidence.

2. A faithful watchman will manifest that he expects to give account by being very careful to know his duty and will take all proper ways that are in his power to become acquainted with it. He will study, as the

apostle directs Timothy, to show himself "approved unto God" (2 Tim. 2:15). He will give attendance to reading, meditation, and prayer and will often call for divine aid on account of his own insufficiency. As a faithful soldier will be careful to understand his duty, so the spiritual watchman will adhere closely to the Word of God for his guide and directory.

3. A minister who watches for souls as one who expects to give account will have none to please but God. When he studies his sermons, this will not be the inquiry, "How shall I form my discourse so as to please and gratify the humors of men and get their applause?" but "How shall I preach so as to do honor to God and meet with the approbation of my Judge?" This will be his daily request at the throne of grace. This will be ten thousand times better than the vain flattery of men. His discourses will not be calculated to gratify the carnal heart; rather he will not shun to declare the whole counsel of God.

The solemn account that the faithful minister expects to give on another day will direct him in the choice of his subjects; he will dwell upon those things that have a more direct relation to the eternal world. He will not entertain his audience with empty speculations or vain philosophy but with things that concern their everlasting welfare. Jesus Christ, and Him crucified, will be the great topic and darling theme of his preaching. If he means to save souls, like a skillful physician he will endeavor to lead his patients into a view of their maladies and then point them to a bleeding Savior as the only way of recovery. The faithful watchman will give the alarm at the approach of the enemy, will blow the trumpet in the ears of the sleeping sinner, and will endeavor to awake him.

4. The pious preacher will endeavor to adapt his discourses to the understanding of his hearers. "He will not be ambitious of saying fine things to win applause, but of saying useful things, to win souls." He will consider that he has the weak as well as the strong, children as well as adults to speak to and that he must be accountable for the blood of their souls if they perish through his neglect. This will influence him to study plainness more than politeness. Also he will labor to accommodate his sermons to the different states or circumstances of his hearers; he will have comforting and encouraging lessons to set before the children of God, while the terrors of the law are to be proclaimed in the ears of the impenitent. He will strive to make distinctions in his preaching, that every hearer may have his portion.

The awful scenes of approaching judgment will have an influence on the Christian preacher with respect to the manner in which he will deliver the message. He will guard against that low and vulgar style that tends to degrade religion; but his language will in some measure correspond with those very solemn and affecting things that do engage his heart and tongue. He will not substitute a whining tone in place of a sermon that, to speak not worse of it, is a sort of satire upon the gospel, tending greatly to depreciate its solemnity and importance and to bring it into contempt. But the judgment will appear so awful, and his attention so captivated with it, that his accents will be the result of a mind honestly and engagedly taken up with a vastly important subject. "Such a preacher will not come into the pulpit as an actor comes upon the stage, to personate a feigned character, and forget his real one; to utter sentiments, or represent passions not his own" (Fordyce).

He does not aim to display his talents. But like one who feels the weight of eternal things, he will not address his hearers as though judgment were merely an empty sound; rather he views eternity as just before him, and a congregation on the frontiers of it, whose eternal state depends upon a few uncertain moments. Oh, with what zeal and fervor will he speak! Death, judgment, and eternity will appear as it were in every feature and every word! Out of the abundance of his heart, his mouth will speak. His hearers will easily perceive that the preacher is one who expects to give account. He will study and preach with reference to a judgment to come and will deliver every sermon in some respects as if it were his last, not knowing when his Lord will call him or his hearers to account. We are not to suppose that his zeal will vent itself in the frightful bellowings of enthusiasm; but he will speak forth the words of truth in soberness, modesty, and Christian decency.

5. They who watch for souls as those who expect to give account will endeavor to know as much as they may the state of the souls committed to their charge, that they may be in a better capacity to do them good. They will point out those errors and dangers that they see approaching; and when they see souls taken by the enemy, they will exert themselves to deliver them from the snare of the devil. The outward deportment of a faithful minister will correspond with his preaching: he will reprove and rebuke, warning his people from house to house. The weighty affairs of

another world will direct his daily walk and conversation in all places and on every occasion.

A Few Particular Addresses

First, to him who is about to be set apart to the work of the gospel ministry in this place:

Dear sir, from the preceding observations you will easily see that the work before you is great and solemn; and I hope this is a lesson you have been taught otherwise; the former acquaintance I have had with you gives me reason to hope that this is the case. You are about to have these souls committed to your care; you are to be placed as a watchman upon the walls of this part of Zion. I doubt not that it is with trembling you enter upon this work. The relation that this day's business has with a judgment to come renders the scene affecting. Your mind, I trust, has already anticipated the important moment when you must meet this people before the bar of God. The good profession you are this day to make is before many witnesses. Saints and wicked men are beholding. The angels are looking down upon us. Above all, the great God with approval or disapprobation beholds the transactions of this day; he sees what motives govern you and will proclaim them before the assembled universe. Oh, solemn and affecting thought! The work before you is great and requires great searching of heart, great self-diffidence and self-abasement. How necessary that you feel your dependence upon God; you cannot perform any part of your work without his help. Under a sense of your weakness, go to Him for help. Would you be a successful minister, you must be a praying, dependent one: do all in the name and strength of the Lord Jesus. Would you be faithful in watching for the souls of men, you must continually watch your own heart. If you are careless with respect to your own soul, you will be also with respect to others'.

Although the work is too great for you, yet let such considerations as these revive your desponding heart. Because the cause is good, better than life, you may well give up all for it. It is the cause of God, and it will prove victorious in spite of all opposition from men or devils: God has promised to be with His ministers to the end of the world, and the work is delightful. Paul somewhere blesses God for putting him into the work of the ministry. The campaign is short, and your warfare will soon be accomplished; the reward is great, and being found faithful, you will receive a crown of glory that fades not away.

Second, we have a word to the church and congregation in this place. My brethren and friends, the importance of the work of a gospel minister suggests the weighty concerns of your souls. As ministers must give account as to how they preach and behave, so hearers also are to be examined as to how they hear and improve. You are to hear with a view to the day of judgment, always remembering that there is no sermon or opportunity that you have in this life to prepare for another world that shall go unnoticed at that decisive court. Your present exercises, with respect to the solemn affairs of this day, will then come up to public view.

God, we trust, is this day sending you one to watch for your souls. Should not this excite sentiments of gratitude in your breasts? Shall God take so much care of your souls and you neglect them? How unreasonable would it be for you to despise the pious instruction of your watchmen! You would therein wrong your own souls, and it would be evidence that you love death. You must bear with him in not accommodating his sermons to your vitiated tastes because he must give account. His work is great, and you must pray for him, as in the verse following the text, where the apostle says, "Pray for us." Since it is the business of your minister to watch for your souls with such indefatigable assiduity, you easily see how necessary it is that you do what you can to strengthen him in this work and that you minister to his temporal wants, so he may give himself wholly to these things. The great backwardness among people in general with respect to this matter at present has an unfavorable aspect. "Who goeth a warfare any time at his own charges? who planteth a vineyard, and eateth not of the fruit thereof? or who feedeth a flock, and eateth not of the milk of the flock?" (1 Cor. 9:7).

Doubtless this man is sent here for the rise and fall of many in this place. We hope he will be used as a mean of leading some to Christ; on the other hand, we tremble at the thought that he may fit others for a more aggravated condemnation. Take heed how you hear.

A Few Words to the Assembly in General Will Close the Subject

What has been said about the character and work of gospel ministers shows us at once that this is a matter in which we are all deeply interested. The greater part of the people present, I expect to see no more until I meet them on the day that has been the main subject of the foregoing discourse. With respect to the characters of the people present, we can say but little about them; only this we may observe—they are all dying creatures, hastening to the grave and to judgment! There must we meet you; there an account of this day's work will come into view; there each one must give account concerning the right discharge of the work assigned to him. The preacher must give account, and you that hear also. Let me say to such as are yet in their sins and proclaim it from this part of the wall of Zion: the enemy of your souls is at hand—destruction awaits you. Oh, flee! Flee to Christ Jesus; bow to His sovereignty. Know this: except you are born again and become new creatures, you cannot be saved.

Shall ministers watch and pray for your souls night and day, and you pay no attention to them? Since they are so valuable, having such a relation to God, if men regarded divine glory, they would regard their souls as being designed to exhibit it. Be instructed, then, to delay no longer, but by repentance toward God and faith in the Lord Jesus Christ make peace with Him before you are summoned before His awful bar. Let me bear testimony against a practice too common on such occasions as this: many people think this a time for carnal mirth and dissipation, than which nothing can be more provoking to God or inconsistent with that day and the strict account that such an occasion tends to excite in the mind. May all, both ministers and people, be exhorted to diligence in their work, that finally we may adopt the language of the blessed apostle: ". . . as also ye have acknowledged us in part, that we are your rejoicing, even as ye also are ours in the day of the Lord Jesus" (2 Cor. 1:14). Amen.

The Important Concerns of Ministers and the People of Their Charge (1797)

Haynes preached this sermon at the funeral of Rev. Abraham Carpenter (1739–1797), founding pastor of a new congregation in the Rutland area in 1788. Carpenter, a strict Congregationalist, served from 1773 in Plainfield's "Whipple Hollow" or "Orange Parish" area of New Hampshire. Carpenter died in September 1797.

This funeral sermon is rare; there are only two known copies, one each at Brown and Howard Universities. It was printed in Rutland, Vermont.

The Important Concerns of Ministers and the People of Their Charge at the Day of Judgment; Illustrated in a Sermon, Delivered at Rutland, Orange Society, at the Interment of The Rev. Abraham Carpenter, Their Worthy Pastor

For what is our hope, or joy, or crown of rejoicing? Are not even ye in the presence of our Lord Jesus Christ at his coming?
— 1 THESS. 2:19

The Second Coming of Christ is a source of peculiar joy and consolation to the people of God; it is a day on which their hopes and expectations will be fully answered. Tribulation attends the good man while in this life; the scenes of Divine Providence are mysterious, and many things are unaccountable and insignificant without a day of judgment; they will then be explained and adjusted, to the joy and admiration of all who love Christ's appearing. Many of the events that take place in this life stand in a solemn relation to the judgment day, and none more so than the gospel ministry; hence it is that the attention of the true servants of Christ is so much taken up with a future state. Paul, being kept away from the church at Thessalonica, sends this epistle as a token of his love and respect to them. In it he anticipates that blessed period when he will meet them at the bar of Christ, which will afford enough joy and satisfaction to more

37

than compensate for all their sorrow, especially his being prevented a personal interview with those to whom he wrote. "For what is our hope, our joy, or crown of rejoicing? Are not even ye in the presence of our Lord Jesus Christ at his coming?" (1 Thess. 2:19). We have two very important ideas suggested in these words. One is that ministers and their people must meet each other at the day of judgment. The second is that although ministers are often separated from their hearers in this life, yet the people of God among whom a pious preacher finishes his work will be a cause or crown of peculiar joy and satisfaction at the Second Coming of Christ.

With respect to the first point, we may observe, to give us a striking contrast between this and the coming world, that we are in the present state subject to many vicissitudes.

What changes are taking place in empires, states, societies, and families! In nothing is this more observable than in matters relating to ministers and the people under their charge. A persecuting spirit that prevailed in the apostolic age was often a means of parting friends, and especially of driving preachers from churches. The same cause has had influence in every age of the church. Though religious societies are happy to escape such a calamity, yet it pleases the Great Head of the church, in His sovereign wisdom, to separate ministers and their people by death. This gives a pious preacher passion and has influence in some degree in every sermon he delivers. That all mankind will be collected before the bar of Christ to see the great and intricate affairs of the universe adjusted is a plain dictate of reason and Scripture, and that many will meet there as having mutual concerns with each other is evident. Especially note that ministers and the people once committed to their charge doubtless will appear in some sense as distinct societies, as each having particular and personal matters to attend to. This supposes that they will have a knowledge of each other, for without this, the purposes of their meeting in such a manner could not be answered. How far this will extend or by what means it will be conveyed is too curious to inquire. It seems that unless we are able by some means to distinguish those from others with whom we have been intimate in this life, the designs of a future judgment will in some measure be frustrated.

The great end of that day is to illustrate divine truth or to make it appear conspicuous to created intelligence. To effect this, God will make use of mankind as instruments. This is the method He takes in this life, and doubtless it will be eligible in the world to come. For our acquaintances to be summoned as witnesses for or against us at this court will perhaps be the best means to administer conviction. In this way the great God can speak in language easy for finite creatures to understand. One design of the world being divided into distinct societies and communities is doubtless to prepare matters for the day of judgment. The relations between ministers and people is such as renders them capable of saying much about each other; in this way the justice and mercy of God will be illustrated, divine proceedings vindicated, and every mouth stopped.

It is our conduct in this life that will direct divine proceeding toward us at the final judgment; that the equity of God's administrations may appear, it is necessary that our characters be clearly investigated. The salvation and damnation of many souls will come through the instrumentality of faithful and unfaithful watchmen; this is an idea contained in the charge God gave to Ezekiel, 33rd chapter. It will be necessary that the motives by which ministers have been influenced in their work be brought into view; for without sincerity of heart they can never execute their office with any degree of true faithfulness and are a high affront to God and a vile imposition on the people.

At the day of judgment the doctrines with which a minister has addressed his hearers must be examined. However widely doctrinal preaching may be discarded by many, and though such words as *metaphysical*, *abstruse*, etc., are often made use of to obstruct free and candid inquiry, yet it is evident that one great end of the gospel ministry is to disseminate right sentiments. Hence it is that Paul so often exhorts Timothy to take heed to his doctrine. Sound doctrine, as well as good practice, is necessary to constitute Christian character. "Whosoever transgresseth, and abideth not in the doctrine of Christ, hath not God" (2 John 9).

A careful inquiry will be made whether an empty parade of learning, elegance of style, etc., have been the main things with which a people have been entertained, tending only to gratify vain curiosity and to fix the attention of the hearers on the speaker. This made Paul condemn such a mode of preaching and "determine not to know any thing . . . save Jesus Christ, and him crucified" (1 Cor. 2:2). Have vague, equivocal expressions been used to convey, or rather to obscure, the truths of the gospel, by which anything and almost everything may be understood? This causes the trumpet to give an uncertain sound and has no tendency to impress or give feeling to the mind, unlike the words of the wise, which are "goads" and "nails" (Eccles. 12:11). Has pleasing men had greater influence on our composing and delivering our sermons than the glory of God and the good of souls? People will be examined at the bar of Christ as to whether they have been dealt with plainly and have been told their characters and danger, that they are wholly opposed to God, destitute of everything that is holy or morally good, that they are by nature under the curse of God's law, exposed every moment to endless woe, that they are hopeless and helpless in themselves, and also the necessity of the renewing influences of the Spirit, the nature of their impotence, consisting in an evil heart, and therefore their being altogether inexcusable and criminal in proportion to the degree of their inability, so that nothing short of repentance toward God and faith in the Lord Jesus Christ is the immediate duty of all who hear the gospel.

Ministers and their people must meet before the judgment-seat of Christ to give an account of whether the true character of God has in any good measure been investigated, as a sin-hating and sin-revenging God. Without this the character of God is kept out of sight, and people are left in the dark and are not able to determine whether they love or hate the true God.

It must be known whether people have had the character and work of the Redeemer set before them—the design of His sufferings, the efficacy of His blood, and the necessity of our union to Him. The manner in which divine truth has been delivered will be a matter worthy of serious examination at that day—whether with that earnestness and fervor becoming the vast importance and solemnity of gospel truth, tending to affect the mind. The deportment or examples of ministers among their people will be closely attended to; their private visits, exhortations and reproofs, holy desires and wrestlings for the souls of their hearers will not escape public notice. The improvement that people have made through such advantages will be brought into public view.

How often people have attended on the ministration of the Word and the manner in which they have done so will be matters of serious concern at the judgment day. Those excuses that men make for neglecting public worship will be weighed on a just scale. Have people contributed to the temporal support of their ministers and so enabled them to devote themselves to the service of Christ, or by great neglect have they obstructed the gospel, robbed God, and wounded their own souls?

It will be useful for the time of a minister's continuance among a people to be known, as that will serve to set the character of gospel despisers in a true point of light. That ministers and the people of their charge will meet each other at the bar of Christ is suggested in my text and in other parts of the sacred writings. It has already been observed that in this way truth will appear conspicuous, and the conduct of God will be vindicated, and the designs of a judgment day will in the best manner be answered. It may further be observed that the matters relating to the gospel ministry are of such magnitude that it is essential that they be attended to, for they concern a judgment day and an eternal state. When ministers and people meet in the house of God, it is an acknowledgment that they believe in a future state of retribution and is a sort of appeal to the day of judgment. The influence of a faithful or unfaithful minister is such as to affect unborn ages; it will determine the sentiments and characters of their successors, and in this way they may be doing good or evil after they are dead, even to the Second Coming of Christ.

That God's hatred toward false teachers, and against those who choose them, together with their criminality, may appear, it will be necessary that these matters be laid open at the tribunal of Christ. As a proof of the matter under consideration, I may only add that there always has been an important controversy, in a greater or lesser degree, between ministers and some of their people. It is so with faithful preachers and some of their hearers; wicked men oppose the doctrines they preach and will not be convinced. Unfaithful preachers have advocates and opposers. The dispute involves the character of Christ; it cannot be settled in this world. How necessary that ministers and people meet at that great day to have the matter decided, the doctrines of Christ vindicated, and the character of ministers or people exonerated.

Another important idea contained in the text is that the church or people of God among whom a faithful minister finishes his work will be a cause or crown of particular joy or rejoicing at the coming of Christ. It will be a matter of great satisfaction to sit down with Abraham, Isaac, Jacob, and other saints at that day; but the Scriptures state that godly ministers will derive particular joy from the pious members of their congregations (Dan. 12:3; 2 Cor. 1:14; Phil. 2:16). Reflecting on past providences will be a source of great joy at the day of judgment; and as many things have taken place between a minister and his people in which they are particularly conversant and interested, when these come to be explained they will afford special joy and admiration. As they have been companions in tribulations, so now it is likely they will be in a special sense co-partners in joy and will help each other magnify the Lord for special favors and displays of divine power and grace on their behalf.

The prayers and struggles of pious teachers have been on behalf of Zion in general and for those over whom the Holy Ghost has made them overseers in particular. God will give them hearers who have been converted through their instrumentality as a kind of reward and fruit of their travail or labor. When it appears that God has made use of the true ministers of Christ for the conversion of some of the souls once committed to their charge, it will excite wonder, joy, and humility in the minds of pious teachers that God should deign to honor them as instruments of such glorious work, by which they will be led to adore sovereign grace and condescending love. As it is often through the painful labors of Christ's servants that souls are brought home to God, doubtless he will approve of such virtues by conferring signal honors on those who have turned many to righteousness, who will shine as stars forever and ever.

Pious people will give an account of their faithful teachers that will meet with the approbation of God, which will be expressed by that heavenly plaudit, "Well done, good and faithful servant" (Matt. 25:21, 23). Their mutual accounts will be given "with joy, and not with grief" (Heb. 13:17). The hopes and expectations of such ministers are great, as the apostle suggests in the text: "For what is our hope, or joy, or crown of rejoicing? Are not even ye?" He speaks of it as the earnest hope and expectation of all Christ's ministers by calling it *our* hope. They reflect with pleasure on the approaching happy moment, and when it comes, it will greatly gratify their holy desires.

That it will be possible to hold equal communion with all the saints at one time in the invisible world perhaps is difficult to grasp. But it appears that the wicked who have been associates in sin here will be companions of torments hereafter (Luke 16:28). They are to be gathered like standing corn and to be bound in bundles to burn. It is more than possible that the righteous who have lived together in this life will have a more intimate access to each other in the world to come.

If it will be useful for ministers and people to meet in some sense as distinct societies, perhaps it will subserve the interest of the universe that they in a degree continue so. It is the character of those in the true church of Christ that they treat His ministers with respect in this life, accounting them as "the ministers of Christ" and "stewards of the mysteries of God" (1 Cor. 4:1). They help them in their work (2 Cor. 1:11). God will in that great day reward people for such kindness, as thereby they express their love to Christ (Matt. 25:40). Recognizing that what has been done to such poor sinful creatures should be taken notice of will gratify the benevolent feelings of Christ's servants and at the same time fill them with holy admiration and deep humility.

Ministers and the people of their charge will assist each other and will be united in bringing a verdict against the wicked and impenitent among whom they lived while on earth. The saints are to judge the world (1 Cor. 6:2). One way by which they will do this will doubtless be to declare before angels and men what they know about them or their conduct in this life. An attachment to divine justice will make this delightful work. Ministers will declare what and how they have preached to them and the bad improvement they have made of the gospel so far as it has come under their observation, how they have despised and mocked the messengers of the Lord and condemned His Word and ordinances. Pious hearers can witness to the same things, and in this way the mutual testimony of godly ministers and people will be strengthened and supported, and divine proceedings against impenitent sinners vindicated. Thus the church will be a crown of joy to her faithful pastor.

Improvement

1. We may infer from this subject that the gospel ministry is of God and that we ought to seek its welfare and use suitable exertions for its support.

Since Scripture and reason dictate that it is so important, especially as it relates to judgment day, we may conclude that God would not do without it, and we may see divine wisdom and goodness in the institution. Nothing is more conducive of divine glory and salutary to men than the preaching of the gospel. Unless these glad tidings are proclaimed, the incarnation of Christ is vain. Nothing but opposition to God and disregard of His glory will make men indifferent to the preaching of the gospel. A rejection of Christ and His ministers generally has vice and open profanity for its inseparable companions. The opposition that the impenitent part of mankind have made to the servants of Christ has doubtless in some measure had its rise from a consciousness that they must meet them at the bar of Christ, to their disadvantage.

2. When a faithful minister is taken away, that ought seriously to be regarded. But there are few ways perhaps by which God shows greater displeasure against a people than in calling His ambassadors home. By this He threatens to put an end to His treaty of peace and become irreconcilable. It may sometimes be the case that God has no more chosen or elect ones among them. When Paul and Barnabas were preaching at Antioch, as many as were ordained to eternal life believed, but then Paul and Barnabas departed (Acts 13). The encouragement for a minister to preach among a people, so far as the salvation of souls ought to be a motive, is the doctrine of election. After the death of a faithful minister there is less hope for a people.

We may further observe, when it is considered that we are to meet them no more in the house of God to hear them declare unto us the words of reconciliation, that our next interview will be at the tribunal of Christ, to hear them testify for or against us. How moving is that consideration! It is more solemn to so die than if we had never been favored with the gospel ministry. People, whether they hear or forbear, shall know, to their joy or sorrow, that there has been a prophet among them (Ezek. 2:5).

3. The subject affords direction on how ministers should preach and how a people ought to hear—namely, with death and judgment in view. It is this that makes preaching and hearing a serious matter and renders the house of God so very solemn. We must soon meet before the bar of Christ, perhaps before the next Sabbath, to have our sermons and our hearing examined by Him who is infinite in knowledge and is present in every congregation. Did we always consider these things, it would tend to abolish that coldness, drowsiness, and indifference that too often attend the ministers of the gospel and that formal spirit that is too apparent among hearers. How that would check the levity of mind and disorderly behavior that presumptuous creatures often indulge in the house of God! "How dreadful is this place!" is a reflection suitable on all occasions, and especially when we meet for public devotion.

4. The surviving widow and children will for a moment suffer a word

of exhortation. Are not you in some sense his hope and joy? Was it not a reflection that tended to smooth the rugged road through death that he would meet you before the bar of Christ and that you would be a crown of rejoicing in that day? If ministers and people are to meet each other before the tribunal of Christ as having special business together, then we may conclude that this will be the case with particular families, such as husbands and wives, parents and children; you can say much about each other upon that occasion, having for so long a time composed one family on earth.

You who are this day called to mourn must give an account how you have improved through his public and more private admonitions, and especially this act of providence. The present occasion, however solemn, will appear more so at the great day. Consider that although he is gone to return no more, yet God, the source of consolation, ever lives. His promises are always new to the widow and fatherless. The God who gave has taken him away. But still he lives in another state and is more useful to the universe than he could be in this world. God's people always die in the best time, manner, and place. You have only time to take up the body and bury it, set your houses in order, and follow him. Manifest your love to the deceased by preparing to meet him and make his heart glad in the day of the Lord Jesus. Contemplate the rectitude of divine government and a future world, and be still.

Let the children remember that to have a pious, faithful parent taken away is an unspeakable loss. Your father has done much for your bodies, but we trust even more for your souls. Never forget his prayers and admonitions. Can you, dare you meet him at the bar of Christ in impenitence? Should this be the case, instead of those endearing and parental caresses that you have received from him in this life, he will join with the Judge of all in saying, "Depart!" He will declare what he has done for you and condemn you. Let your mother experience that tender regard and kind assistance during her short continuance with you as becomes dutiful, obedient children. Make her heart glad by a holy life, and let your father live daily before her eyes in your pious examples.

Let me say a word to the church and congregation in this place. Dear friends, I am not a stranger to these mournful sensations that the present melancholy providence tends to inspire. I trust I am a hearty mourner with you and a sharer in your loss.

By the foregoing observations you have reason to conclude that you have lost a faithful minister. You can't forget those solemn and affectionate warnings that he has given you from the pulpit, nor those pious examples he has set before you. He has preached his last sermon. Your next meeting must be before the tribunal of Christ, where those sermons you have heard him deliver in this life will come to view, and also the improvement you have made because of them. Will you, my brethren, be his crown of rejoicing in that day? If you were his hope and joy in this life, you doubtless are still. It is with satisfaction, we trust, that at this moment he looks forward to that day when he expects to see the dear people once committed to his charge; doubtless he hopes to meet some of you as crowns of rejoicing. Oh, do not disappoint the hope and expectations of your reverend pastor. Manifest your love to him by imitating his holy example and by keeping those heavenly instructions that he so often inculcated always in remembrance and by preparing to give him joy in the day of the Lord Jesus. Examine what improvement you have made of the gospel ministry while you had it, and whether too great inattention has not had influence in its being removed.

Have you ever experienced the power and efficacy of the gospel upon your own souls? Have you by the Holy Spirit been formed into the moral likeness of the blessed God and into the image of His Son Jesus? Or have you been content with the mere form of godliness? Have you, through sloth and unbelief, neglected attending on the preaching of the gospel during the residence of your pastor among you? Oh, what account such gospel despisers will have to give another day! Consider, I entreat you, how dreadful it will be to have these things brought into view when you come to meet your minister, who was once and perhaps is now an eyewitness of your conduct and will testify against you to your everlasting condemnation!

Your minister, though dead, now speaks. He preaches a most solemn lecture to us all on mortality this day.

You will, as it were, hear his voice when you look on the place of public worship where he and you so often attended, when you look on his grave here among you, and when you look to the Second Coming of Christ. Think often of that day. Let the Sabbath and worship of God be still dear unto you. Remember him who has spoken unto you the Word of God, and follow his faith.

The Sufferings, Support, and Reward of Faithful Ministers, Illustrated (1820)

Published in Bennington, Vermont in 1820, this is Haynes's dramatic farewell sermon to the Rutland congregation he served for thirty years. Sixty-five years old and beleaguered by constant conflicts with various members over church discipline, this was nonetheless a moment of mixed emotions for Haynes. Recalling 1,500 Sabbaths and 5,500 sermons led him to confess, "I did not realize my attachment to you before the parting time came."

The Sufferings, Support, and Reward of Faithful Ministers, Illustrated. Being the Substance of Two Valedictory Discourses, Delivered at Rutland, West Parish, May 24th, A.D. 1818.

> *But none of these things move me, neither count I my life dear unto myself, so that I might finish my course with joy, and the ministry, which I have received of the Lord Jesus, to testify the gospel of the grace of God.*
>
> — ACTS 20:24

Long and painful experience evinces this truth: the present world is in a state of suffering, and its influence is as extensive as the inhabited globe. The fall of man points out its commencement and duration. No age, country, or character can plead exemption. The gifts, grace, and inspiration of the great apostle of the Gentiles could not deliver from this calamity, though he could recapitulate scenes of distress as well as anticipate troubles yet to come. Ephesus was the metropolis of what is called the minor Asia. Paul visited there in the year 53 and preached for three years; but on account of dissensions and persecutions he departed and went to Troas, and from thence to Macedonia and Corinth, proposing to embark for Syria at Cenchrea, which was about nine miles from Corinth, on its eastern boundary. But he feared the Jews, who understood his course and the fact that he was carrying money to Jerusalem, which he had collected for the saints. When they lay in wait to rob and kill him, he altered his course and returned to Macedonia. He visited many churches and came to Miletus, several miles to the south, where he sent for the elders at Ephesus, that he might have an interview with them. To them he gave the valedictory address contained in the chapter from whence my text is selected. The people at Ephesus were acquainted with the particular trials of their former minister, which might excite sympathetic and distressing feelings, and perhaps tend to dishearten them in the cause of religion.

To fortify their minds against such discouragements, the holy apostle gives them to understand that he was not in the least intimidated or turned aside from advocating that cause that he had heretofore inculcated at Ephesus and elsewhere. This sentiment is expressed in the heroic and ecstatic language of the words before us: "But none of these things move me, neither count I my life dear unto myself, so that I might finish my course with joy, and the ministry which I have received of the Lord Jesus, to testify the gospel of the grace of God."

The method I propose in illustrating the subject before us is:

I. To show that ministers of the gospel receive their commission from the Lord Jesus Christ.

II. That they will soon accomplish their work and finish their course.

III. That wherever they go they may expect to meet with trials and sufferings.

IV. That they ought not in the least to fear or be moved from the path of duty by their trials but persevere in their work.

V. That the faithful ministry of the servants of Christ will terminate or issue in their great joy and satisfaction.

I. To show that ministers of the gospel receive their commission from the Lord Jesus Christ.

Paul says in my text that he received it of the Lord Jesus Christ. The same apostle is very explicit on this subject: "But I certify you, brethren, that the gospel which was preached of me is not after man. For I neither received it of man, neither was I taught it, but by the revelation of Jesus Christ" (Gal. 1:11-12). Again, "How shall they preach, except they be sent?" (Rom. 10:15). "No man taketh this honour unto himself, but he that is called of God, as was Aaron" (Heb. 5:4). In the early periods of time, preachers of righteousness were called and sent forth by the Almighty. In every succeeding age God has been carrying on his work by the ministry of men, and such are called prophets, apostles, etc. It was through the instrumentality of gospel ministers that the Kingdom of the Redeemer was promulgated in the days of the Messiah, who gave them their commission and sent them forth upon the important embassy (see Matt. 10:26; Luke 10:3). Although many of the early bishops were called in a miraculous and extraordinary manner, this by no means suggests the idea that ordinary ministers do not receive their commission from God and are not equally sent by Him.

The appropriate names belonging to the ambassadors of Christ illustrates the sentiment before us. They are called stewards, servants of the Most High, ambassadors, etc. These characters involve the idea of negotiating business for others and of receiving commission from them. Plenipotentiaries are invested with full power to act by the court that sends them. Angels are sent from heaven to be ministering spirits on earth and so in this sense bear a relation to the servants of Christ.

The faithful ministers of Christ are engaged in the cause of God, and it seems suitable that He should appoint them. They are messengers sent on the King's errand, to transact business for Him and receive their commission from above. They come to people in the name of the Lord. The motives by which the faithful ministers of Christ are influenced to enter upon their work are not congenial with the natural and carnal dispositions of men; no wicked man, while in that state, is disposed to be a pious preacher of the gospel. So when any are so inclined, they are moved thereto by the Holy Ghost. When Paul engaged in this work, he had to contend with a fleshly and selfish heart; he did not confer with flesh and blood (Gal. 1:16). All the natural, spiritual, and acquired abilities that ministers possess are from God. And He directs outward circumstances, by which a door is opened for their usefulness and improvement. When Paul came to Troas to preach, he observed that a door was opened to him by the Lord (2 Cor. 2:12). The gospel ministry was an ascension gift of Christ (Eph. 4:8).

Faithful ministers derive strength from Christ to preach and discharge ministerial duties. They are taught to go to Him for help and can exclaim in the language of a pious preacher, "I can do all things through

Christ which strengtheneth me" (Phil. 4:13). They can say, "the Lord stood with me, and strengthened me" (2 Tim. 4:17).

Ministers receive directions from Christ *how* and *what* to preach. They are to preach the message that God tells them to (Jonah 3:2), with *plainness* or clarity. The trumpet is to give a distinct and certain sound. They are also to deliver God's messages with *earnestness*, with a sense of the importance of their work. Jonah was to cry against Nineveh. Isaiah was to cry aloud and spare not, lifting up his voice like a trumpet. Those awfully betray their trust who deliver their discourses in a cold, formal, and lifeless manner, as though death, judgment and eternity, and the souls of men are things to be trifled with. Paul could tell the elders of Ephesus that he had not shunned to declare unto them all the counsel of God (Acts 20:27), that he had kept back nothing that was profitable to them (v. 20).

The servants of Christ are directed by Him how long to tarry with a people. The dispensations of Divine Providence dictated to Paul that after a three-year continuance at Ephesus, it was time to leave them. He who sent forth the first evangelists gave them this direction: "And whosoever shall not receive you, nor hear your words, when ye depart out of that house or city, shake off the dust of your feet. Verily I say unto you, It shall be more tolerable for the land of Sodom and Gomorrah in the day of judgment, than for that city" (Matt. 10:14–15). Verse 23 adds, "But when they persecute you in this city, flee ye into another." Jeremiah was directed by God to terminate his ministry among his people. "Therefore pray not for this people, neither lift up cry nor prayer for them, neither make intercession to me: for I will not hear thee" (Jer. 7:16). There was a time when the ministry of Hosea with Israel was to cease. He was to let them alone (Hos. 4:17).

The usefulness of a minister among a people may appear to be at an end. This may be occasioned by the unfaithfulness of ministers, the people, or both; there is criminality somewhere. It may be the case that people make violent attacks on a minister's character and do all they can to destroy his influence and come forward with the hypocritical plea, "The man's usefulness is at an end" and so cloak their wickedness and deceit under the garb of religion. The great clamor and hue and cry against the church and against servants of Christ is from high pretenses to sanctity, and you will find that those who make the widest mouths in their vociferations are the most destitute of virtue and religion.

II. It was proposed to show that ministers will soon accomplish their work and finish their course.

Paul speaks in my text of finishing his course. We are all on a journey, traveling into another world. This is the case with ministers in common with other men. They are not able to continue by reason of death (Heb. 7:23). As the word *dromos* ("course") signifies, they have an object in view, on which their attention should be fixed, even on the things that are eternal (2 Cor. 4:18).

The prophets, apostles, and eminent servants of Christ who give us daily instruction—where are they? Do they live forever? No. They ran their race, they finished their course, and their work on earth among the people once committed to their care has come to an end. Paul pursued his work with diligence and rapidity, like one in a race. He visited many places and planted churches in seven towns in Italy, in Greece nine, in Syria nine, in Asia Minor ten, in Asia fifteen, in Egypt three. He visited seventeen islands. It is said that he was converted on the 25th day of January and was baptized the 28th. In nine years he traveled 1,928 miles. He preached much in Arabia. On a second journey he went 1,744 miles. His third was 2,154 miles. His fourth was 3,396 miles.

He traveled much more after this. Paul is supposed to be about seventy years of age when he died. He calls his life only a moment and says that "the time is short" [1 Corinthians 7:29]. The lives of ministers are often shortened by the trials with which they meet; sometimes they are actually put to death for the sake of the gospel. They can say with this holy apostle, "As dying, and, behold, we live; as chastened, and not killed; as sorrowful, yet always rejoicing" (2 Cor. 6:9-10). The memory of a Patrick, Beveridge, Manton, Flavel, Watts, Doddridge, Edwards, Hopkins, Bellamy, Spencer, and Fuller is precious to us; but alas, we see them no more. No more in their studies; no more the visitants of their bereaved flock; no more in their chapels or sanctuaries on earth. Their successors in office are pursuing them with rapid speed and will soon, very soon, accomplish their work. The labors of faithful ministers subject them to pulmonary and many other diseases common to public speakers. Instruments there are on every side to hurry them to the bar of God and put an end to their labors. So with propriety they may adopt the language of dying Peter: "Shortly I must put off this my tabernacle" (2 Pet. 1:14). Since I came to this state [Vermont], which is a little more than thirty years, twenty-seven ministers have died on this side of the Green Mountain, and altogether forty have been dismissed from their people; two lie dead in this burying yard. Paul lived nine or ten years after delivering his farewell discourse. Moses continued his ministry for eighty years, Noah for 120, Jeremiah for thirty-two years. But oh, how soon they finished their course and bid farewell to the world!

III. Wherever ministers go, they may expect to meet with trials and sufferings.

This was what was taught by Paul through the Holy Ghost, as you will see in the two verses immediately preceding my text: "And now, behold, I go bound in the spirit unto Jerusalem, not knowing the things that shall befall me there: save that the Holy Ghost witnesseth in every city, saying that bonds and afflictions abide me" (Acts 20:22-23). We are taught by the same Spirit that "we must through much tribulation enter into the kingdom of God" (Acts 14:22). Our blessed Lord, when He sent out His disciples to preach, let them know that they went forth like sheep among wolves (Matt. 10:16). Ezekiel's hearers were as uncomfortable and tormenting as thorns and briars that tear and wound the flesh; he was so hedged in that he could have no access to their minds or any influence among them. The wicked are compared to a hedge of thorns (Prov. 15:19). God says of people, "Behold, I will hedge up thy way with thorns" (Hos. 2:6). It is the case with sinners that they are so prejudiced against the doctrines of the gospel and the servants of Christ that it is dangerous to come near them. What a sore complaint was made against Jeremiah's hearers: "Their tongue is as an arrow shot out; it speaketh deceit: one speaketh peaceably to his neighbour with his mouth, but in his heart he layeth his wait" (Jer. 9:8).

If we trace the dispensations of Divine Providence further, we obtain further evidence in proof that the servants of Christ may expect to meet with trials wherever they go. Paul went to Arabia, and the Jews sought to kill him. He went to Jerusalem, Judea, Syria, Cilicia, and most of the countries of Asia Minor, and his sufferings increased. We have a catalog of them in the sketches he gives of his life. He observes, "We are fools for Christ's sake" (1 Cor. 4:10). Paul suffered in name and reputation. Defaming him by propagating falsehood and lies was not uncommon.

People had the impudence and boldness even to slanderously report that he and others said, "Let us do evil, that good may come" (Rom. 3:8). In Acts 17:18 he is called a "babbler." "*Babbler* is used by the critics as a term of utmost contempt, an allusion to a little worthless chattering bird, that used to pick up the seeds which were scattered in the market place" (Dr. Guyse). They pretended he was a man who had picked up a few scraps of "learning, in different places, of which he wanted to make a show; and as one who was fond of hearing himself speak, even among those who had studied more than he had" (Dr. Scott). "The tongue of a Tertullus is uncommonly eloquent, (though some more gifted in lying, says one) when called to calumniate Paul before a Roman Tribunal. He begins, says Beza, by a diabolical rhetoric, and flattery, and ends with lies." In Acts 24:5-6 we read, "For we have found this man a pestilent fellow, and a mover of sedition among all the Jews throughout the world, and a ringleader of the sect of the Nazarenes: who also hath gone about to profane the temple: whom we took, and would have judged according to our law."

Lying about the ministers of Christ has been a common thing. "Being defamed, we entreat: we are made as the filth of the world, and are off-scouring of all things unto this day" (1 Cor. 4:13).

> We are become the purgation of the world. The learned observe, that the persons who were sacrificed to the Gods for averting their anger and for procuring deliverance from any public calamity, were called *purifiers*, and were commonly very mean worthless persons, and at the time of their being sacrificed were loaded with execrations: that all the misfortunes of the state might rest upon them. The word signifies *expiation*. The apostle compares himself to those devoted persons, who were sacrificed for the purpose above mentioned. The filth of all things. The word signifies filth scoured off: to scour off all around. It is used most commonly to denote the sweeping of the streets, and stalls, which being nuisances are moved out of sight as quick as possible. (Dr. Macknight)

Dr. Scott observes, "They were held as the filth of the world, and refuse and scum of the earth. They were considered below contempt: or as worthy of execration as pestilence and nuisance: who ought to be purged, or extirpated out of society, as the common sewer carries away the filth and off-scouring of the city, to prevent infection and disease. Like human victims, peculiarly mean and vile, offered to the infernal Gods, with vehement expressions of abhorrence and execration."

Paul's enemies thought him to be the fruitful source of their calamities, and could they only be rid of him, their troubles would cease, their gods would be at peace with them. The united cry was, "Away with such a fellow from the earth; for it is not fit that he should live" (Acts 22:22). It was a perilous event with this holy apostle when he was with "false brethren" (2 Cor. 11:26). Hear a detailed account he gives of his sufferings:

> In labours more abundant, in stripes above measure, in prisons more frequent, in deaths oft. Of the Jews five times received I forty stripes save one. Thrice was I beaten with rods, once was I stoned, thrice I suffered shipwreck, a night and a day I have been in the deep; in journeyings often, in perils of waters, in perils of robbers, in perils by mine own countrymen, in perils by the heathen, in perils in the city, in perils in the wilderness, in perils in the sea, in perils among false brethren; in weariness and painfulness, in watchings often, in hunger and thirst, in fastings often, in cold and nakedness.
>
> — 2 COR. 11:23-27

It was not the least of his trials that those who professed friendship to him and to the cause of religion became traitors and his enemies. How painful was the reflection of the pious apostle to think that many of the Galatians, who had given recent expressions of friendship to him, had so awfully departed from the truths of the gospel and had become inimical to him! Consider his affectionate expostulations:

> I am afraid of you, lest I have bestowed upon you labour in vain. . . . Ye know how, through infirmity of the flesh, I preached the gospel unto you at the first. And my temptation which was in my flesh ye despised not, nor rejected; but received me as an angel of God. . . . Where is then the blessedness ye spake of? for I bear you record, that, if it had been possible, ye would have plucked out your own eyes, and have given them to me. Am I therefore become your enemy, because I tell you the truth?
>
> — GAL. 4:11, 13-16

When vindicating the cause of God against opposers, he complains that *all* forsook him at first (2 Tim. 4:16). When the professed friends of God forsake the ministers of Christ, it is attended with circumstances especially aggravating. The sweet council and communion they have taken together is now interrupted, mutual confidence destroyed, the parties exposed to peculiar temptations, which renders it difficult to retain that forgiving spirit manifested by the holy apostle when all men forsook him: "I pray God that it may not be laid to their charge."

David, the man after God's own heart, was tried in this particular way. "For it was not an enemy that reproached me; then I could have borne it: neither was it he that hated me that did magnify himself against me; then would I have hid myself from him: but it was thou, a man mine equal, my guide, and mine acquaintance. We took sweet counsel together, and walked unto the house of God in company" (Ps. 55:12-14). Above all, when the professors of religion take sides with the world against the servants of Christ, they strengthen the hands of the wicked, and the Savior is wounded in the house of his friends, which must excite painful sensations in the hearts of faithful ministers. The history of the preachers of the gospel in every age of the world affords distressing evidence in proof of the point before us. The imprisonment of a Rutherford or a Baxter, the sufferings of a Manton, Flavel, Whitefield, and their contemporaries, evince this truth that opposition to the servants of Christ is not an accidental thing but is kindred with the corruption or depravity of the human heart.

To carry on their opposition against Paul, friendship to the gospel or to the doctrines he preached was pretended. They claimed that it was not religion or his preaching that excited their dissatisfaction but the character of the man, and could they be rid of him, they could be advocates for the same sentiments. Thus attachment to the cause of Christ was the motive by which they professed to be influenced. They would therefore employ and hear men who preached Christ with a design to carry their point against Paul and render him contemptible. "Some indeed preach Christ even of envy . . . not sincerely, supposing to add affliction to my bonds" (Phil. 1:15-16).

The wretched and dangerous state of unconverted sinners is another source of distress to the faithful servants of Christ. This caused "great heaviness and continual sorrow" in the heart of Paul (Rom. 9:2). He was lamenting the torments of hell, says Mr. Leigh in his *Critica Sacra*. The history of Moses, David, and the prophets—yea, of the blessed Savior of the world—affords painful demonstration in proof of the point under consideration.

All gospel ministers know experimentally, in some degree, "the terror of the Lord" and are led to "persuade men" (2 Cor. 5:11). The man who does not appreciate the worth of souls and is not greatly affected with their dangerous situation is not qualified for the sacred office. It was the saying of a pious minister who would arise at midnight for prayer, "How can I rest, how can I sleep, when so many of my congregation are exposed every moment to drop into hell!" The ambassadors of Christ have been called to sacrifice their property, ease, reputations, yea, their lives for the salvation of men's souls. Like Paul they suffer the loss of all things, not counting their lives dear unto them, being driven from town to town, and "have no certain dwelling-place" (1 Cor. 4:11). The requitals or returns made to the apostle for his benevolence to men and his sacrifices for their good were bitter ingredients in the cup of affliction. He was cast among beasts at Ephesus to be torn in pieces and carried the scars of the whip on his back; and the more faithful, the more hated and abused he was, and the less beloved (2 Cor. 12:15).

The consequences that often attend a minister's leaving a people are distressing. God frequently gives such people up to divisions and carnal dissipation, to heresy, and to an awful contempt for divine institutions. Or if the externals of religion are attended to, it is often merely to keep themselves in countenance and to support a reputation among men; they often sink into a state of mere formality. Oh, how troubling to a pious minister it is to see his flock that was the delight and joy of his heart and once committed to his charge become an easy prey to the enemy of their souls! How bitter was this reflection to our apostle. "For I know this, that after my departing shall grievous wolves enter in among you, not sparing the flock. Also of your own selves shall men arise, speaking perverse things, to draw away disciples after them" (Acts 20:29-30).

The analogy between cause and effect suggests the idea that the servants of Christ may expect to meet with trials and opposition wherever they go. They will continue to preach the same soul-humbling doctrines, perhaps with greater and greater degrees of perspicuity and zeal; they will still testify to the grace of God; they will have the same kind of hearers, whose hearts are in enmity against God; and so they may expect to meet with similar treatment. Paul preached the same gospel at Jerusalem, Macedonia, Rome, etc.

In a word, there is no place in this world where either ministers or people can find a peaceful asylum; it is compared to the rolling sea:

No, 'tis in vain to seek for bliss:
For bliss can ne'er be found,
Till we arrive where Jesus is,
And dwell on heavenly ground.

IV. In following the method proposed, I aim to show that whatever trials the servants of Christ meet with in finishing their course, they ought not to fear or be moved out of the path of duty but persevere in their work.

"None of these things move me." That is, "I look on them as mere trifles and make no account of them."

Paul did not account even his life dear unto him. He argues from the greater to the less. If the dearest thing, even life, was of no value compared with the cause of God, how diminutive were those afflictions that lasted only for a moment, especially when we consider that gospel ministers suffer in obedience to the commands of God. "And thou, son of man, be not afraid of them, neither be thou afraid of their words, though briars and thorns be with thee, and thou dost dwell among scorpions; nor be dismayed at their looks, though they be a rebellious house" (Ezek. 2:6). "Be not afraid of their faces: for I am with thee, to deliver thee, saith the LORD" (Jer. 1:8). "Then spake the Lord to Paul in the night by a vision, Be not afraid, but speak, and hold not thy peace: For I am with thee, and no man shall set on thee to hurt thee" (Acts 18:9-10). Jesus said, "And I say unto you, my friends, Be not afraid of them that kill the body, and after that have no more that they can do" (Luke 12:4). Obedience to the commands of God will as effectually secure His people from eventual harm as the high and unyielding walls of the New Jerusalem will the inhabitants of heaven.

The examples of Him who spoke as never man spoke should be a powerful incentive to encourage His servants in their work (1 Pet. 4:1). With what persevering diligence did He execute His ministry in the face of earth and hell until, in dying accents, He could exclaim, "It is finished." The cause in which ministers of Christ are engaged may well excite them

to persevering faithfulness and fidelity in their work. It is that dear interest for which all things were created, the cause of the ever blessed God
in three persons, for which the glorious Redeemer shed His precious
blood and is now pleading, a cause to which all the dispensations of
Divine Providence are subservient, and in which all the forces of heaven
are engaged. The character, oath, life, yea, all the perfections of the Deity
are pledged for its defense. "Lo, I am with you always, even unto the end
of the world. Amen" (Matt. 28:20) is a promise that to all faithful ministers, at all times, even to the Second Coming of Christ, is as replete with
encouragement and support as can be given by the pen of inspiration.

By being steadfast and immovable under trials, the servants of God
can bear an honorable testimony in favor of religion. This is one way
by which God has furnished the advocates of the gospel with particular
arguments in defense of the truth and has made them rejoice and glory
in tribulation. It is not a stoical apathy that reconciles God's people to
sufferings; it is not because they are not susceptible of injuries or are
ignorant of abuse. But God is glorified by their patiently enduring. That
is why the language of the persecuted apostles was so appropriate. Acts
5:41 says, "And they departed from the presence of the council, rejoicing that they were accounted worthy to suffer shame for his name." Our
blessed Lord told His disciples, "Blessed are ye, when men shall revile
you, and persecute you, and shall say all manner of evil against you
falsely, for my sake. Rejoice, and be exceedingly glad: for great is your
reward in heaven: for so persecuted they the prophets which were before
you" (Matt. 5:11-12).

The ministers of Christ are frail, imperfect creatures in common with
other men. They need thorns in the flesh to humble them and keep them
low; and their afflictions tend, if patiently endured, to work for them an
exceeding "weight of glory" (2 Cor. 4:17). One reason Paul was so useful
to the church of God was on account of his being a vessel chosen and
formed in the furnace of affliction. Perhaps more accurate attention to
order would have led me to an additional detail regarding the sufferings
of God's people under a former head, such as a body of death, of which
Paul so much complained, making him cry out, "O wretched man that I
am!" [Romans 7:24]. I believe this is the greatest enemy with which faithful ministers have to contend, and it excites the most painful sensations.
Oh, the pride, the stupidity, the corrupt passions, the selfishness that

they often feel, tending to draw their minds away from God and divert them from a close adherence to duty. These are trials that cleave unto us, go where we will. They are too apt to be intruders even into our solemn acts of devotions, like Abraham's fowls descending to mar the sacrifice [Genesis 15:11], and it is hard to drive them away.

Ministers of the gospel need not be moved from the path of duty or be discouraged under suffering because it is what they may reasonably expect. This was suggested by Christ to the first preachers, to fortify them against despondency (John 16): "These things have I spoken unto you, that ye should not be offended. They shall put you out of the synagogues: yea, the time cometh, that whosoever killeth you will think that he doeth God service" (vv. 1-2). And, "But these things have I told you, that when the time shall come, ye may remember that I told you of them" (v. 4).

The ambassadors of Christ have sworn to be faithful. They are all under oath; and for them to betray their trust is treason and high-handed perjury. Their profession is before many witnesses: "I give thee charge in the sight of God, who quickeneth all things, and before Jesus Christ" (1 Tim. 6:13). What is a life, yea, ten thousand lives, when contrasted with what is sacrificed by our deserting the cause of God? The great and sure reward promised to the faithful servants of Christ for all their sufferings will more than barely support them amidst all the sorrows of life. Every pain, every tear, every insult they bear for Christ's sake will secure them a great reward in heaven (Matt. 5:12). The wearisome and tiresome nights they spend here in running their race and in finishing their course will only prepare them for a more sweet repose and rest at their journey's end when the morning shall break forth.

V. The faithful ministry of the servants of Christ will terminate or issue in their great joy and satisfaction: "so that I might finish my course with joy."

1. They will have the approbation of their own consciences. "For our rejoicing is this, the testimony of our conscience, that in simplicity and godly sincerity, not with fleshly wisdom, but by the grace of God, we have had our conversation in the world, and more abundantly to you-ward" (2 Cor. 1:12). It leads to a holy triumph, says Guyse. Conscience will not be an idle or indifferent spectator at the day of judgment; it will have its own influence in accusing or excusing in the day "when God shall judge the secrets of men" (Rom. 2:15-16). It will be a source of unspeakable

torment to the wicked, a gnawing worm that will never die; but where its dictates have been held sacred and not violated, peace, comfort, and holy rejoicing will be the attendants. The true friends of God amidst all the calumny cast upon them by men and devils can say in the face of a frowning world, "we trust we have a good conscience" (Heb. 13:18).

2. When godly ministers have finished their course, all their imperfections and trials will end. They see so many defects in themselves, so much self-seeking, unfaithfulness, and ignorance, that they often tremble lest after they have preached to others, they themselves may be cast away, that they shall fall short of that heaven they have so often recommended to others and have their dwelling with the wicked. But these fears will subside, and to their surprise they will hear their Redeemer say, "Enter thou into the joy of thy lord!" (see Matt. 25:21, 23).

All those sorrows, caused by the state of impenitent sinners, that have occasioned them many wearisome days and nights will forever cease. No more slander, no more stripes or imprisonments. They will be out of the reach of men and devils, will obtain a complete and everlasting victory, and will shout that ecstatic song, "I have fought a good fight, I have finished my course" [2 Tim. 4:7].

3. God will explain to them those things that now appear dark and intricate: why so much distress, why they must be made the song of the drunkard, why they must be driven from town to town and have no certain dwelling-place. The providences of God will all appear harmonious, calculated through divine ordination to promote the highest glory of the universe and their personal good. "Who shall not fear thee, O Lord, and glorify thy name? for thou only art holy . . . for thy judgments are made manifest"—this will be their song forever (Rev. 15:4).

4. It will afford special joy to the people of God, especially to ministers of Christ, when they have finished their course, in that God will publicly plead and espouse their cause and will vindicate the doctrines they inculcate according to truth. The enemies of religion often complain that preachers set forth strange things, that they are too rigid, too pointed and overbearing in their preaching, tending to wound the delicate feelings of their hearers, like goads and nails (see Eccles. 12:11). There is no stopping the wide mouths of gainsayers; but so far as ministers have been faithful, God will acknowledge them and will vindicate their cause against the vile aspersions of wicked men. Their character will be exoner-

ated and cleared from those "hard speeches" that ungodly sinners have spoken against God and His people (Jude 15).

5. The sentence that will be pronounced and executed on the wicked will bring joy to the saints. In this world the ministers of Christ often tremble by anticipating the misery that is coming upon sinners, and especially on their hearers who disregard their admonitions and reproofs. Like their divine Lord and Master, they weep over them. But at the day of judgment, although pain and misery will in themselves be considered undesirable, yet their holy and perfect attachment to the divine character will render the displays of vindictive justice glorious and will excite praise and adoration. "Rejoice over her, thou heaven, and ye holy apostles and prophets; for God hath avenged you on her" (Rev. 18:20).

6. The great and unspeakable reward and honor that will be bestowed and conferred on the faithful servants of Christ will be a matter of great joy. It will exhibit the condescending grace of God and excite humility in them; they will scarcely believe that God could ever take notice and reward such poor services as they have done and will cry out with wonder, love, and praise, "Lord, when saw we thee an hungered and fed thee? or thirsty, and gave thee drink? When saw we thee a stranger, and took thee in? or naked, and clothed thee? Or when saw we thee sick, or in prison, and came unto thee?" (Matt. 25:37-39). As God's rewarding the saints will humble them, so it will tend to fit them for the world of everlasting adoration. One great design of the day of judgment will be to exhibit the riches of divine grace, which will excite endless songs of joy to the saints.

The more thy glories strike mine eyes
The humbler I shall lie;
Thus, while I sink, my joy shall rise
Unmeasurably high.

—ISAAC WATTS.

God will make it evident that those who had trials of cruel mockings and scourgings, of bonds and imprisonments, who were stoned and sawn asunder, tempted, slain with the sword, who wandered about in sheepskins and goatskins, in deserts, on mountains, and in dens and caves of the earth, being destitute, afflicted, tormented, were men, after all, "of whom the world was not worthy" (Heb. 11:36-38).

The scars and signs of sufferings in the cause of God that His people will carry with them will procure more illustrious monuments than pillars of marble. They will possess the Kingdom prepared for them and will be made kings and priests unto God. This was that dignity to which Paul was aspiring, the prize of the high calling, that for which he did not account his life "dear" or honorable unto him [Acts 20:24]. The Greek word here is *timios*, "honorable, precious."

Finally, it will enhance the joy and reward of the ministers of Christ to meet all their brethren and companions in tribulation. There will be so great a degree of similarity in the sufferings of the servants of God and in the interpositions of Divine Providence toward them as to excite a pleasing and holy fellow feeling in their souls. The celestial spark will catch from breast to breast, while a harmonious flame of divine love and adoration will ascend as from one to Him who has given them all the victory. Ministers will meet the pious part of their congregations with great rejoicing, especially those to whom they have been instrumental in saving good. Such will be ministers' own crown of rejoicing in the day of the Lord Jesus (2 Cor. 1:14; 1 Thess. 2:19-20; Heb. 13:17).

Paul will meet with his brethren that were at Corinth, Rome, etc. A more public and interesting rehearsal of their mutual and personal interviews will be attended to. What reciprocal joy will his meeting with Timothy and his son Onesimus afford! The parting of the apostle and his Ephesian brethren at Miletus was painful and distressing—what weeping and sorrowing! But at their arrival at the haven of eternal rest, what a contrast! No fearing that they will see each other's faces no more. That once mournful parting, and Paul's valedictory sermon, is recognized with emotions of joy as an event necessary to promote the further promulgation of the gospel and to accomplish the decrees of heaven.

Ministers and their people when they have finished their course will remember those Bethel visits that they have enjoyed in the sanctuary and around the Table of the Lord and the sweet counsel they have taken together. They will remember the seasonable reproofs given to each other, and whatever differences have taken place between them will all be forgiven and forever exterminated. They will see the wisdom and goodness of God in all these things. Thus when the ministers of Christ have finished their course, that will put an end to all their troubles; and so their ministry will end or issue in their unspeakable joy and consolation.

Improvement

1. Since ministers receive their commission from Christ, none have any right to forbid them from preaching. All courts of inquisitions, all prohibitory measures adopted by men to prevent their declaring the glad tidings of the gospel or fulfilling the ministry they have received from the Lord Jesus, is an insult to the majesty of heaven, reveals a spirit hostile to religion and the rights of men, and ought to be treated with a holy contempt by all servants of Christ. With what religious indignation were those presumptuous measures treated that were used to stop the mouths of those recorded in Acts 4. "And they called them, and commanded them not to speak at all nor teach in the name of Jesus. But Peter and John answered and said unto them, Whether it be right in the sight of God to hearken unto you more than unto God, judge ye. For we cannot but speak the things which we have seen and heard" [vv. 18-20]. Again, in chapter 13, when the Jews opposed Paul and Barnabas, they "waxed bold" in their work [v. 46].

2. Since ministers receive their commission from heaven, we see the obligations that people are under to regard them and to pay attention to the sacred lessons they are to inculcate. To reject and despise the ambassadors of Christ is very dangerous. To do so insults the sacred Trinity and is accounted high treason in the court of heaven. It indicates the displeasure of the king when ambassadors are abused and recalled; the treaty or negotiation of peace is closing (2 Chron. 36:16). People have mocked the messengers of God and despised his words and misused his prophets, until the wrath of the Lord arose against them, until there was no remedy. Let the enemies of God fear and tremble when they read the credentials of Christ's ministers, sanctioned with this solemn inscription: "He that heareth you heareth me; and he that despiseth you despiseth me; and he that despiseth me despiseth him that sent me" (Luke 10:16).

3. Ministers must soon finish their course, and that thought should excite them to the utmost faithfulness, constancy, and focused involvement in their work, seeing their time is short. Paul reminded his Ephesian brethren that for the space of three years he ceased not to warn everyone night and day with tears. The same apostle exhorted Timothy to give attendance to reading, exhortation, and doctrine (1 Tim. 4:13).

It is desirable for the servants of Christ to receive such a decent support as to be able to devote all their service to the sanctuary and the souls of their hearers. Every sermon should be a kind of farewell discourse. It is said of the pious Mr. Shepherd that he used to say that he never preached a sermon but what he thought it might be the last. Oh, how it becomes us to preach and act like dying men, that we may finish our course with joy!

4. It is no evidence that ministers are not the true servants of Christ because they meet with great opposition from the world, and even from the professors of religion. Yea, it is from the high pretenders to sanctity that the Savior of men suffered most severely. Paul observes concerning bishops that they "must have a good report of them which are without" [1 Tim. 3:7]. Did the apostle mean by this to prove that he himself was disqualified from the sacred office, being of bad report among the enemies of God? This above all others would disqualify Christ Himself for the ministry. He observes to those whom He sent forth as preachers, "Blessed are ye, when men shall hate you, and when they shall separate you from their company, and shall reproach you, and cast out your name as evil, for the Son of man's sake" (Luke 6:22). And, "Blessed are ye, when men shall revile you, and persecute you, and shall say all manner of evil against you falsely, for my sake" (Matt. 5:11). That the ambassadors of Christ should so conduct themselves as to give no just occasion to those who are outside the church to reproach the cause of God is evident. Doctor Macknight offers the following paraphrase on 1 Timothy 3:7: "Moreover, before his conversion he must have behaved in such a manner as even to have a good testimony from the heathen, that he may not be liable to reproach for the sins he committed before his conversion, and fall into the snare of the devil, who, by these reproaches, may tempt him to renounce the gospel, knowing that he has little reputation to lose." The heathen may more willingly receive him if he was formerly a man of good reputation. We are assured that this verse was never designed to fix a reproach on the character of the faithful servants of Christ or to sanction those invectives and slanders so often cast on them by the enemies of God.

That the Word of God is often wrested and perverted by him who is no stranger to the art and introduced his evil machinations is evident, even from the farce he attempted with the blessed Savior of the world, even saying, "It is written." It is far from being a singular case to have people make and spread false and scandalous things concerning the ministers of the gospel, and even to offer rewards to such as will join in their game, and then to accomplish their designs by having the audacity and duplicity to say, "The man is of bad report among those who are outside the church." Was not the Savior of men betrayed in this way?

5. Since ministers receive their commission from the Lord Jesus Christ, it is dangerous for them to go before they are sent. It is suitable that they have some exterior evidence of their mission, something more than their pretensions to inward sanctity. Early extraordinary ministers could exhibit miraculous testimonials of their being called to the sacred office. It seems equally necessary that in all succeeding ages the ambassadors of Christ have some kind of credentials to show their being called to the work. We therefore find that ordinary ministers not only appeared to be inwardly called by the Holy Ghost or were in the judgment of charity good men, endowed with ministerial gifts and graces, but were recommended and set apart by those in office and ordained by the laying on of hands. Those, therefore, who thrust themselves into the work without these prerequisites do not come in by the door appointed by the great head of the church but climb up some other way and ought not to be treated and encouraged as true ministers of Christ.

6. Since all true ministers receive their commission from the court of heaven, there ought to be a cordial union among them: they should treat each other as brethren. Although they may have differing gifts, the strong are not to despise the weak. They derive their ministry from the same authority, bearing the same signet. They are called by different names, such as bishops, overseers, ministers, elders, etc. But we do not conceive that these are expressions of superiority or diversity of grades in office, any more than various names among men imply different species. The soldiers of Jesus, deriving their commission from the same king and being engaged in the same cause, should as far as possible see eye to eye and strengthen each other's hands.

7. We infer the truth of the Holy Scriptures that so accurately foretell the trials and sufferings of good ministers. The benevolent embassy with which they are entrusted and the authority with which they are invested would seemingly indicate better treatment, were it not confronted by predictions in the sacred volume. While therefore the enemies of God slander and persecute the servants of Christ, they in a degree establish the truth of divine revelation.

8. The subject of Christian ministry teaches us how to account for the firmness and intrepidity discovered by the people of God, especially the ministers of Christ, in every age. They will not give up the cause, come life or come death. This rendered Luther, Melanchthon, Hus, Jerome, Polycarp, Wycliffe, and a thousand others invincible to all the flatteries and intrigues of wicked men and devils, and even the menaces and terrors of an inquisition. They could say, "None of these things move us."

9. There will be a very solemn meeting of ministers and people at the day of judgment. Joy and terror will attend the transactions of that day. Ministers and people will meet as having special business with each other; their reciprocal conduct will be publicly investigated. How suitable that these things are seriously examined with candor now, before the commencement of that day.

As in the course of Divine Providence a dissolution of the pastoral and ministerial relation between me and this people has lately taken place, according to the declaration of an ecclesiastical council convened for that purpose, I have been requested to deliver a valedictory discourse. As I am still residing among you, the occasion is different from the one that took place between Paul and those he was then taking his leave of. He told them that he knew that those among whom he had been preaching the kingdom of God would see his face no more. This may or may not be the case with this speaker. I am willing to say something on this occasion, which I esteem solemn and interesting, hoping that I shall be enabled to address you with all the plainness and prudence that become one who expects to give an account. The apostle reminded the Ephesian brethren of some things that had transpired while he was with them.

My brethren and friends, the church of Christ in this place was organized on the 20th day of October forty-two years ago by the assistance of the Rev. Benajah Roots, my worthy predecessor.

It was thirty years ago the 28th day of March since I accepted the pastoral care of this church and people. The church then consisted of forty-two members; since which time, about 312 have been added to it, about sixty have been removed by death, and about 400 have died in this society, including those above mentioned. There are only ten of the church now living in this place who were here when I first came among you; the greater part sleep in death. I have preached about 5,500 discourses; 400 of them have been funeral sermons. I have solemnized more than 100 marriages. During this period we have had two remarkable seasons of the outpourings of the Spirit, as well as some refreshings at other times, which many of us who are yet alive recognize with emotions of joy. Twice I have been brought, in my own apprehensions, to the borders of the grave; but God has spared me to see this day of trial, which I desire to meet with resignation to His will.

The flower of my life has been devoted to your service, and while I lament a thousand imperfections that have attended my ministry, yet if I am not deceived, it has been my hearty desire to do something for the salvation of your souls. He that provided the motto of our discourse could say on his farewell, "I have coveted no man's silver or gold or apparel. Yea, you yourselves know that these hands have ministered unto my necessity." The appropriation of such language is in a degree in concord with the testimony that many present could give and might be admitted were it not for the danger of comparison. I have sometimes thought that perhaps God designated that I should spend my few remaining days among you, and with a degree of satisfaction I have looked into the repository of the dead adjoining this house, intending to sleep with them, claiming a sort of kindred dust, and intending to rise with them. But the ways of God are mysterious, and He often destroys the hope of man. In my solitary reflections I cast a look toward this house, to bid it a final adieu. But in spite of all that fortitude dictated by reason and religion, the sympathetic tear will betray the imbecility of human nature. Can we suppose that even a Paul was unmoved when "they all wept sore, and fell on his neck . . . sorrowing most of all . . . that they should see his face no more" (Acts 20:37-38)?

A three-year ministry had excited reciprocal endearments that made the parting like tearing soul and body asunder. More than 1,500 Sabbaths have I spent with you, most of them in this house. More than 130 seasons of Communion have we enjoyed around the Table of the Lord. Oh, how many sweet and comfortable days have I spent in this house with you who are alive and with those who are dead! We have taken sweet counsel together. I trust I have at times felt the powerful presence of Christ while speaking from this desk. Cannot we adopt the language of the poet Isaac Watts:

> 'Tis with a mournful pleasure now
> I think on ancient days;

Then to Thy house did numbers go,
And all our work was praise.

It appears in the course of Divine Providence that my labors among you have come to an end. We have finished meeting together in this house. I am called to give you the parting hand. But let us all remember that a very solemn meeting awaits us at that day suggested in my text, when we shall all have finished our course.

Our meeting at that day will greatly differ from what it has been in this house. I have often been here and found but few within these walls. Some trifling excuse has detained you; but at that day it will not be optional with people whether they attend or not, for all will be there. The congregation will be full; not one in a town, state, or the world will not appear. Sometimes you have manifested great dullness, and I have witnessed drowsiness and carelessness while I have been speaking. But at that day you will be awake and will be all attention. You will believe, realize, and feel interested in the things exhibited. Often through the depravity of the human heart and the prejudice that sinners have toward the truth and the servants of Christ, they will turn their backs on divine worship and leave the house of God. But when ministers and people meet before the tribunal of Christ, there will be no deserting or quitting the assembly. There they must hear, however disagreeable the preaching will be and tormenting to their consciences. In this house our meeting has been indiscriminate; saints and sinners sit on the same seat. Around the same table we cannot certainly say who is and who is not wearing the wedding garment. But at the day of judgment there will be an exact separation—Christ will separate the sheep from the goats.

In this house we have often met, not less than four thousand times; we go and we come. Although we see no fruit of our labor, we do not wholly despair—we hope God may yet bless His word. But when ministers and people meet before the bar of God, it will be the last interview, with none to follow it. The case of sinners will then be forever hopeless and helpless.

One great design of our meeting together in this world is to offer salvation to sinners, to entreat and beseech them to be reconciled to God. But at the day of judgment an irreversible sentence will be rewarded, and sinners condemned and sent to endless perdition.

When the ambassadors of Christ have finished their course and meet their people, a critical examination will take place. I must give an account concerning the motives that influenced me to come among you and how I have conducted myself during my thirty-year residence in this place—the doctrines I have inculcated, whether I have designedly kept back anything that might be profitable to you or have, through fear of man or any other criminal cause, shunned to declare the whole counsel of God. Also, I must answer as to the manner of my preaching—whether I have delivered my discourses in a cold, formal manner—and my external deportment. You who have been the people of my charge must give an account of what improvement you have made through my ministry—whether you have attended as you ought, whether your excuses for withdrawing from public worship at any time were sufficient. God will attend to them, and they will be weighted in a just balance; not a single neglect will escape divine notice. Our thousand excuses, when put in the scale of the sanctuary, will be lighter than a feather.

You must give a strict account regarding the manner of your attending in this house—whether you have received the Word with joy and obeyed its precepts. Parents must render an account—whether they have taught their children by precept and example to reverence the Word of God and to respect the servants of Christ, whether they have endeavored to maintain or support the influence of their minister among the youth or rising generation and so have been workers together with him, whether the servants of Christ fall into contempt in a measure through their instrumentality. People will be examined whether they have contributed to the temporal support of the ministers of Christ. It will not be left with men how much they ought to impart. God will be the judge of how much was suitable and whether it was agreeable to the Word of God and the exigencies of the preacher.

There are often criminal causes for the separation of a minister from his people, either on the part of the minister or the people or both. To escape censure, there may be pretended reasons to keep the truth out of sight. Ecclesiastical councils may think it inexpedient to make any inquiry into the matter; but they will have a plain, candid, and thorough investigation before the tribunal of Christ. No deception, no hypocrisy will be concealed under religious pretenses; it will all be detected and exposed before the assembled universe, and the hearts of all men will be revealed.

> *Nothing but truth before his throne,*
> *With honor can appear:*
> *The painted hypocrites are known*
> *Through the disguise they wear.*

—ISAAC WATTS

Accusations brought against the ministers of Christ will be examined. Ministers will fare no better for the name they sustain; their wickedness will be exposed. They will be condemned or exonerated, not according to popular noise and clamor, but according to truth and equity. These are scenes, my brethren, that are opening before us and to which we are hastening with the utmost rapidity. These are things that should move us and call up our attention. It is a small, very small, thing to be judged by man's judgment. Oh, let us labor to be found by God in peace. This day to me in some respects is very solemn and interesting, a day on which I am called to give you the parting hand. But its importance is eclipsed when contrasted with that awful period when we are to meet before Him who will judge the quick and the dead.

There you and I must shortly appear. Much has been said on the subject of my dismissal, that it has been in consequence of my request. I think I have been sufficiently explicit on the matter; but I am willing to repeat it in this public manner: had the people been united, wholesome discipline properly exercised, a firm and unshaken attachment to the cause of God manifested among all the professors of religion, I should have chosen to have continued with you, at the expense of temporal advantage. But considering the existing divisions and the prevalent uncommon stupidity, I have been fully satisfied that it was my duty to be dismissed, and I have requested my friends not to oppose it. I am persuaded that it will be seen another day that unfaithfulness in the minister, to the exclusion of criminal causes in this society, did not originate the event. But this matter is laid over to the day of final decision. I trust I feel in a degree reconciled, knowing that God's way is in the sea and in the deep waters, and his footsteps are unknown.

I find my strength in a degree inadequate to itinerant labors, and I am shortly to put off my tabernacle. But I purpose, so long as life and health continue, to preach the same gospel that I have been proclaiming to you for more than thirty years and on which, I humbly hope, I have ventured my eternal salvation. Oh, that I may be enabled to discharge the duty with greater zeal and fidelity! And now I am called to go, not to Jerusalem, but from place to place, not knowing the things that shall befall me, saving what the Holy Ghost and the providence of God witness in every city—namely, that trials await me. But I hope I can in some small degree say, "But none of these things move me, neither count I my life dear unto myself, so that I might finish my course with joy, and the ministry, which I have received of the Lord Jesus, to testify the gospel of the grace of God" [Acts 20:24].

My dear brethren and friends, I did not realize my attachment to you before the parting time came. Many disagreeable things have taken place, but still I feel my heart going out toward this people. How many pleasant days have I spent with you in this house? How many hours under your roofs, and how many delightful visits in your families? I cannot think of one door that has not been hospitably opened for my reception. Many kindnesses have I received from you, both in sickness and in health. You will accept my warmest gratitude for the many instances of kindness shown me. I hope, my dear brethren and sisters in the Lord, that you will still remember me at the throne of grace—that God would support me under every trial, that He would render the evening of my life useful to the church of God, that utterance may be given unto me, that I may open my mouth boldly to make known the mystery of the gospel.

May the great head of the church send you a pastor after his own heart, vastly superior in gifts and grace to him who is giving you his farewell address. It is distressing to think that I am about to leave any of you in an unconverted state, that my labor among you will prove to your heavier condemnation. Particularly let me call on you who are young—this house and your own consciences are witnesses that I have repeatedly called on you to attend to the important concerns of your never-dying souls, but I fear that for too many of you it has been in vain. Have you not turned a deaf ear to the calls and invitation of the gospel and to the solemn warnings of God in His providence? I fear you are going down to eternal destruction, under the intolerable weight of aggravated sins. I will now, perhaps for the last time, invite you to Jesus, the God-man and Mediator. Some of your parents on a deathbed have charged me with their dying breath to be faithful to you. Should it appear at our meeting at the day of judgment that I have in any good measure answered their request, must I re-echo to the tremendous sentence of the Judge, "Depart!"? Oh, how dreadful, how heart-rending the anticipation! Must this be the case? Nothing but a speedy and thorough repentance and turning unto God can prevent it. Dear youth, your souls were once committed to me, and I would now commit them to Him who is able to keep you from falling and to present you faultless before the presence of His glory with exceeding joy.

In general you have treated me with respect. I do not remember ever receiving an insult from a single youth. Many of your parents sleep in the dust, where I must shortly be. Should I be so happy as to sit down with them in the kingdom of heaven, and should you arrive to those blissful regions, oh, what a blessed exchange! With what ecstatic joy and congratulation should we present the offering before the throne of God, with the humble, grateful, and astonishing exclamation, "Here, Lord, we are, and the natural and spiritual children You have graciously given us!"

You will shortly hear of the death of the speaker. Whether his grave will be here or elsewhere is uncertain. Oh, remember that those icy fingers were once employed in writing sermons for you. Those lips that are now chained in gloomy silence were once speaking to you in accents that were sounding from Sabbath to Sabbath and from year to year within the walls of this house. His soul has taken its flight to yonder tribunal, where a rehearsal of these discourses that you have heard from him will be made in your ears and before the assembled universe. Ministers who have finished their course may be useful to people after they are dead. This idea was suggested by a dying apostle (2 Pet. 1:15). Moreover, I will endeavor that you may be able after my decease to have these things always in remembrance. How far, consistent with truth and Christian modesty, I may adopt the language of the holy apostle will be better known hereafter: "Wherefore I take you to record this day, that I am pure from the blood of all men. For I have not shunned to declare unto you all the counsel of God" (Acts 20:26-27).

It was for your sake principally that your fathers called me here. They sat under my ministry but a short time; their memory is still precious, and though dead they still speak. Oh, for their sake and for your soul's sake and above all for the sake of Him who created you, hearken to the things that concern your eternal interest. Could you consider your former minister worthy of any respect, I beseech you to manifest it by preparing to meet him and to be a crown of his rejoicing in the day of the Lord Jesus. You who are young will be those who will compose this society within a short time; we who are advanced in life must soon leave you.

Let me warn you against Sabbath-breaking, against neglecting the public worship of God. Willingly and promptly contribute to the support of the gospel ministry if you would prosper in this world and meet your Judge in peace. Beware of carnal dissipation, a sin that I have often warned you against. Beware of slander and condemnation, those banes of society, to which influence, even among us, you cannot be strangers. According to Scripture's testimony, they have their origin in hell (Jas. 3:6) and are marked with characters not very ornamental to human nature; nor do they stand fair candidates for the kingdom of heaven. "Know ye not that the unrighteous shall not inherit the kingdom of God? Be not deceived: neither fornicators, nor idolaters, nor adulterers, nor effeminate, nor abusers of themselves with mankind, nor thieves, nor covetous, nor drunkards, nor revilers, nor extortioners, shall inherit the kingdom of God" (1 Cor. 6:9-10).

Suffer me to warn you against false doctrines, such as are pleasing to the carnal heart. The inventions of men are skillful in exciting prejudices against the plain truths of the gospel: hence it is that faithful ministers are accused with being too pointed and unpolite in their discourses. Beware of false teachers and of being led astray by the errors of the present day. Remember these are damnable *heresies* as well as damnable *practices*. Paul predicted this danger: "For I know this, that after my departing shall grievous wolves enter in among you, not sparing the flock" (v. 29). "But, beloved, we are persuaded better things of you, and things that accompany salvation, though we thus speak" (Heb. 6:9). Dear children, lambs of the flock, you have in a sense for a time been committed to my care. With the tenderest affection I would, in the arms of faith, bear you to that divine Savior who has said, "suffer the little children to come unto me, and forbid them not: for of such is the kingdom of God" (Mark 10:14; Luke 18:16). May your cheerful hosannas fill this house when your fathers and mothers shall sleep in the dust.

My friends in general, whatever we have seen amiss in each other, it becomes us to exercise forgiveness, as we hope God, for Christ's sake, has forgiven us, and as we would find mercy in that day. How often have our united prayers ascended up in this house; may we not forget each other in time to come. Live in peace, and may the God of peace be with you. May my family who have been brought up among you have a share in your affections and intercessions; they will doubtless soon be left without parents. May the wife of my youth, who has been my companion in tribulation, whose health and strength and domestic ease have been sacrificed and devoted to your service, should she survive me, not be forgotten. As I still continue to reside among you, should you at any time be destitute of a minister on a sickbed, be ready to send for me. It will be the rejoicing of my heart to do all I can to comfort you in the hour of distress and to facilitate the groans and terrors of a dying moment. I request the same from you as there is opportunity.

And now, brethren, I commend you to God and to the word of his grace, which is able to build you up and to give you an inheritance among all them who are sanctified. Amen.

PART TWO

Bishop Daniel A. Payne:
A Vision for an Educated Pastorate

Daniel Alexander Payne was born February 24, 1811 to London and Martha Payne, free blacks in Charleston, South Carolina during the height of slavery. Devout members of the Methodist Episcopal Church, the elder Paynes committed young Daniel to the service of God through prayer even before Daniel was born. Immediately following Daniel's birth, his father had him dedicated at the family church and returned home where he prayed that the boy would grow up to serve the Lord. Hence Daniel remarked that he was "thrice consecrated" to the work of the Lord.

However, London Payne did not live to see the fulfillment of his hopes. Six months after his son's fourth birthday, London died. At age nine and a half Daniel lost his mother as well. After his parents' death, Daniel's great-aunt raised him and instructed him in the faith.

Despite hardships associated with racial castes in South Carolina and the loss of both his parents, young Payne proved intellectually curious and industrious. While not the custom or the law to educate blacks in the antebellum South, Payne found the means to assemble piece by piece an education replete with classical studies. At age eight he began studies with the Minors' Moralist Society, an organization established by free blacks to "educate orphan or indigent colored children, and also to provide for their necessary wants."[1] After two years of instruction in that

Society, Payne received three years of tutelage from Thomas S. Bonneau, whom he described as the most popular schoolmaster in the city. While with Bonneau, young Payne studied reading, writing, "ciphering as far as the Rule of Three," and the histories of Greece, Rome, and England. At age twelve Daniel ended his studies with Bonneau and held apprenticeships with a local shoe merchant, a tailor, and a carpenter for the next five years. During his stint with the carpenter, which lasted about four and a half years, Daniel applied himself to learning Latin, Greek, and Hebrew and "every book within [his] reach."

By age fifteen the intellectual fervor shown for history, classics, and works of science turned to spiritual matters. "I . . . felt the Spirit of God moving my childish heart" and "was often led by the Spirit to go to the garret to bend the knee and look up into heaven, beseeching the Lord to make me a good boy."[2] Daniel applied to the Methodist Episcopal Church and was accepted as a probationer with that body. However, Payne recalled that his conversion did not take place until three years later at the age of eighteen. "I . . . gave Him my *whole heart*, and instantly felt that peace which passeth all understanding and that joy which is unspeakable and full of glory." Several weeks after his conversion, Payne received an "irresistible and divine" impression during an afternoon prayer. A voice spoke to him saying, "I have set thee apart to educate thyself in order that thou mayest be an educator of thy people."[3] Thus began Daniel Alexander Payne's lifelong mission to improve the educational condition of his people.

At age nineteen Payne flung himself into his newfound calling. Leaving the carpenter's trade, he opened his first school in 1829 with three children and three adult slaves for a monthly income of three dollars. Unable to support himself after a year, Payne closed and later reopened his school with redoubled commitment and a larger facility. The school rapidly outgrew its quarters and "became not only the largest but by far the most influential school for the education of colored people in Charleston, if not in the entire South."[4] From 1830 to 1835 the school and its leader flourished. The school grew to some sixty pupils. Payne, the young autodidact, squirreled away every cent to purchase texts and made use of every beneficence from sympathetic and wealthy whites to further his pursuit of knowledge. Adding to his earlier studies with Bonneau and the Minors' Moralist Society, he mastered studies in geography, botany, chemistry, philosophy, astronomy, and French well enough to incorporate them into his school's regular course of instruction.

But on April 1, 1835 the experiment in educating free and enslaved Africans came to an abrupt halt when the South Carolina General Assembly passed *Act No. 2639, An Act to Amend the Law Relating to Slaves and Free Persons of Color*. That Act prohibited any person from teaching or causing any slave to read or write and sanctioned free white transgressors with a fine up to $100 and six months' imprisonment, free persons of color up to fifty lashes and fifty dollars, and slaves fifty lashes. As if addressing Daniel Payne directly, the Act specified that if "any free person of color or slave shall keep any school or other place of instruction for teaching any slave or free person of color to read or write, such free person of color or slave shall be liable to the same fine, imprisonment, and corporal punishment as are by this Act imposed and afflicted upon free persons of color and slaves for teaching slaves to read or write."[5]

Lutheran Theological Seminary, Gettysburg, Pennsylvania (1863).
Payne began attending the seminary in 1835 and in June 1837 received a
ministerial license from the Lutheran Church. Courtesy: Library of Congress.

Sleepless, loaded with disappointment, failing in prayer, and doubting the existence and justice of God, Payne closed the school on March 31, 1835 and shortly thereafter moved north from South Carolina to New York. While in New York Payne received encouragement to obtain further education and training at the Lutheran Theological Seminary in Gettysburg, Pennsylvania. His stay in New York lasted some ten days before he moved to Gettysburg in April 1835. In June 1837, after initially resisting any call into full-time Christian ministry, Daniel Alexander Payne was licensed by the Lutheran Church and was fully ordained about two years later by the Synod at Fordsboro, New York. He was a little over twenty-six years old.

In the winter of 1841 he joined the African Methodist Episcopal Church (AME) and by 1843 was received into full connection with that body. It was as a pastor and later as a bishop of the AME that Payne's contribution to the Christian church was most felt. In particular, Payne's tireless efforts to reform the character and educational quality of the African-American pastorate earned him the moniker "Apostle of Education to the Negro as well as the Apostle to Educators in the AME Church."[6]

Daniel Alexander Payne almost single-handedly changed the educational culture and expectations of pastors and preachers in the AME Church. In 1843–1844, shortly after receiving ordination, Payne published a series of five "Epistles on the Education of the Ministry." The "Epistles" met strong denouncement from most AME preachers. Presenting his plans for instituting a course of study for ministerial education at the 1844 General Conference, Payne was summarily voted down by a large majority of the attendees. However, with the intervention of several prominent and influential leaders, his resolution passed unanimously the following day, and Payne was made chair of a newly created Committee of Education assigned with defining a proper course of studies for young preachers. The committee outlined a two-year course for exhorters and a four-year course for preachers that would shape the future character of the AME pulpit and pastorate.

Francis Grimké summed up the state of the church thus: "Up to this time, any ignoramus who imagined that he was called to preach, who thought that the Lord had need of him, felt that it was his right to be ordained, or at least to be licensed; and no objection was interposed by the church, under the impression that if a man opened his mouth the

Lord would fill it." Following the educational reform efforts of Payne, "the church was now firmly committed to the policy of intelligence as against ignorance in the pulpit. Its aim henceforth would be, not only to see that the Gospel was preached, but that it was done by men who had had, at least, some intellectual preparation for it."[7]

The work of Rev. Daniel A. Payne had only begun at the 1844 General Conference. From 1845 to 1850 he labored as pastor of Baltimore's Bethel Church. In 1848 the General Conference appointed him historiographer of the church and unsuccessfully attempted to persuade him to serve as a bishop. From 1850 to 1852 Payne vacated the pastorate and focused on traveling to finish his history of the AME Church. Finally, at the 1852 General Conference, despite his earlier attempts to evade the post, Daniel Alexander Payne's peers elected him bishop of the New England Conference. Payne recalled:

> I trembled from head to foot, and wept. I knew that I was unworthy the office, because I had neither the physical strength, the learning, nor the sanctity which makes one fit for such a high, holy, and responsible position. . . . I prayed earnestly that God would take away my life rather than allow me to be put into an office for which I felt myself so utterly unfit.[8]

From this concern over his own fitness, one may discern Payne's exalted esteem for the ministry and calling of pastor and bishop. His was not a case of making much of himself and his learning while regarding his brothers lightly. He evaluated himself with the same seriousness by which he judged others. In his view the undereducated and ill-prepared minister was a scandal and affliction upon black churches.

The cause of education, seemingly snuffed out by the South Carolina General Assembly, found a wider audience and platform inside the AME Church. Upon election as bishop, Payne turned his sights on both the education of ministers and the education of lay members of the church.

> In 1844-45, when I wrote and sent abroad my thoughts on education, I had not the power to enforce them, but in my episcopal capacity what was formerly only advice to be given became a duty to be performed. Two things I found necessary to be done. The first was to organize literary and historical associations among and of the ministers, to improve the ministry; the second, to improve the people. An educated ministry

is more highly appreciated by an educated laity, and hence always better supported. They act and react upon each other.[9]

With this dual focus on ministers and their people, Bishop Payne began organizing Mothers' Associations to aid women in the training of their daughters. In 1856 he led the AME Church in securing and dedicating Wilberforce University to the "grand work of Christian education" and served for thirteen years as the university's first president. Wilberforce was the first institution of higher education owned and operated by African-Americans. Payne served as the school's president from 1863 until 1876. A consummate educator, Bishop Payne continued regular writing activities following his tenure at Wilberforce, including publication of *Treatise on Domestic Education* (c. 1885), his autobiography *Recollections of Seventy Years* (1888), and *History of the AME Church* (1891).

Wilberforce University, Xenia, Ohio (The Colored Peoples College).
Drawn, lithographed, and printed in oil colors by Middleton Wallace & Co (1850–1860).
Courtesy: Library of Congress.

In 1847 Daniel Payne wed Julia A. Farris, a widow from Washington, D.C. Married for only one year, Julia died hours after giving birth to a daughter. The daughter died nine months later. In 1854 Payne married his second wife, Eliza Clark, who had one adult and two minor children at the time of the marriage. The oldest, a stepdaughter, married within a year of Payne's marriage to her mother and died approximately three years later.[10] At the age of eighty-two, Daniel Alexander Payne himself died on February 24, 1911.

The sermons and addresses included in this volume are representative of Bishop Payne's emphasis on the education, preparedness, and Christian character of the minister of God. In each of the selections something of the bishop's vision for reforming the educational character of both the minister and the congregation stands out. The three offerings cover twenty-two years of Bishop Payne's service, demonstrating his career-long concern for the integrity of the gospel ministry.

At the General Conference of 1852, Daniel Payne received from Bishop Morris Brown a last-minute request to provide the conference's opening address. Payne proved "instant in season, out of season" (2 Tim. 4:2) as he selected 2 Corinthians 2:16 and the theme "Who Is Sufficient for These Things?" Perhaps the text indicated Payne's four-year-long resistance to and fear of being chosen as a bishop, but it also provided a short outline for a preacher's calling as Payne saw it. First, the preacher is to preach the gospel. That vocation did not consist of "loud declamation and vociferous talking" or "whooping, stamping, and beating the Bible and the desk" or seeing who "hallooes the loudest and speaks the longest." Preaching the gospel, according to Payne, required acquainting man with the holy God of heaven, with man's just condemnation, with his need for the Savior, and with the necessity of repentance and faith. Second, a faithful minister cultivates maturity in the flock and thereby "train[s] them for usefulness and for heaven." Third, a good pastor disciplines and governs the church. This difficult duty requires the pastor "to make his flock intimately acquainted with the doctrines of the Christian Church, instruct them in the principles of Church government, reprove them for negligence and sin, admonish them of their duties and obligations, and then try and expel the obstinate, so as to keep the Church as pure as human wisdom, diligence and zeal, under divine guidance, can make it."

Payne could rightly ask along with the apostle Paul, "who is sufficient for these things?" These tasks—preaching the gospel, cultivating Christian maturity in the congregation, and exercising biblical church discipline—were only possible by fusing an educated mind with true Christian experience and piety while depending wholly on the sufficiency of God. The one who is sufficient for the life and work of the ministry is the one who "lives the life of faith and prayer" and who seeks to fill "his head [with] all knowledge and his heart with all holiness" in pursuit of his Lord.

In 1859 Bishop Payne authored an essay for the Literary and Historical Society of the Missouri Conference entitled "The Christian Ministry: Its Moral and Intellectual Character." Using 2 Timothy 2:1-2, he expounded at great length the moral and intellectual character demanded of the minister of Jesus Christ. Morally, teachers of Christianity are to be faithful men, firm in their adherence to the truth. Words, conduct, charity or love, sincerity and earnestness of spirit, faith, and purity display the moral character of Christian ministers. Men failing in these qualities were judged by Payne to be better suited for the hog pen than for the pulpit. Intellectually, the faithful pastor or minister is characterized by an ability to teach others, not mistaking the *desire* to teach for the *ability* to do so. The unsearchable riches of Christ are to be entrusted only to men with improvable minds, an unquenchable desire for useful knowledge, the ability to apply God's Word, sound judgment, aptness to teach, and humility rooted in a correct knowledge of one's self and a deep sense of one's own unworthiness. The Christian minister is to dedicate himself to cultivating the life of the mind. He is "to *feel* and *know* that he was not to be a mere drone about the hive, a snail in the garden, or a lounger about the house of God—but that he had a mind, and that mind was made for *thinking, investigating, discriminating—for study*." As bishop, Payne insisted that all candidates for the ministry be examined for these qualities.

> Whenever a young man comes forward, and tells us that he is called to the ministry, let us examine him rigidly, according to our excellent discipline and the requisitions of God's word. It is not enough that he tells us God has called him; let him show the evidences of his call. Some of us are too credulous. If a man tells us that he is called to this work, we believe without proof; without any qualification, we are ready to push him into the sacred office. His say so is not enough.

Payne concluded, "Some men have gifts, but no graces. Others have graces, but no gifts. Neither of these are wanted in the Christian ministry." "The Christian Ministry: Its Moral and Intellectual Character" called Christian ministers to make sure they possessed both the giftedness and the graces necessary for this high call.

"The Divinely Approved Workman" (1874) is perhaps this volume's clearest statement of Bishop Payne's understanding of the life of study required of the servant of Christ. Here Payne gives attention to the subject and sources of study and to the shame that befalls any minister neglecting these duties. The source of study was always to be God. Payne encouraged his hearers to study God as He revealed Himself in four sources: nature, history, man, and supremely in Scripture. Failure to consider God in the study and to comprehend His character from all available sources results in the shame of the spiritual workman. Payne concluded that such a workman needs to be ashamed both of his ignorance and of his vices. And yet the educational and moral preparedness of the minister is not to be the only concern of ministers. Payne challenged the local church to be deeply involved in the education of all people of color. He called the local church to prepare men and women for careers in education, to send young men to Wilberforce for preparation for ministry, and to educate young women for Christian work in the community and the home.

> Perhaps there is no greater power in a given community than that of educated women. I use the term in its broadest, highest sense, by which I do not mean a smattering, or even excellence in music, instrumental and vocal, in drawing and painting; nor do I mean a mere classical or scientific and mathematical training. But I do mean a Christian education, that which draws our head and heart toward the Cross, and after consecrating them to the Cross sends the individuals from beneath the Cross with the spirit of Him who died upon it, sending them abroad well fitted for Christian usefulness, a moral, a spiritual power, molding, coloring community, and preparing it for a nobler and higher state of existence. . . .

It could be said that Bishop Payne saw the divine workman as one who fits his own mind for the task of fixing other minds on Christ and His work. He envisioned a Christianity with educating power—instructing and enlightening in areas religious, moral, intellectual, civic, and political. His example and his teachings, challenged as he was by every disadvantage of slaveholding society and racial prejudice, leave for us who have no excuse an immense responsibility for improving our own minds and the life and minds of those the Lord entrusts to our pastoral care.

Bishop Daniel A. Payne, from the frontispiece to his autobiography, *Recollection of Seventy Years* (Nashville: AME Sunday School Union, 1888).

Who Is Sufficient for
These Things? (1852)

Payne delivered this opening address at the General Conference of 1852 at the last-minute urging of Bishop Morris Brown. Payne would be elected bishop at this general conference.

Who is sufficient for these things?

—2 COR. 2:16

To comprehend the meaning of the apostle in these words, it is necessary to remember that the cause of his writing the first epistle to Corinth was the existence of certain evils in the church therein located, such as the dissensions growing out of a preference on the part of some for Paul, of others for Apollos, of a third class for Cephas, and of a fourth class for Christ; also the incestuous person who had married his own father's wife. After reproving them for the first, he commanded them to cure this latter evil by excommunicating the transgressor. Then after rebuking their spirit of litigation, along with every other prominent evil among them, he showed them the structure of the church of Christ, briefly alluded to the manner in which this church was to be governed, and then closed with a graphic description of the glorious results of the death and resurrection of Christ. But in this, the second epistle, he seems to have written for the restoration of the incestuous person, who had heartily repented of his sin and gave proof of this by an utter abandonment of his evil way. Paul then compared the law of Moses with the glorious gospel of Christ, showed his faithfulness and diligence in preaching it and his power as an apostle to punish obstinate sinners, and concluded with a general exhortation and prayer. From all of this it is evident that the ministry of the gospel and church government were the themes that filled up his vision when he exclaimed in the language of the text, "Who is sufficient for these things?" Do not our hearts respond, "Who is sufficient for these things?" To consider these things as clearly and yet as briefly as possible is our duty on this occasion, and may the Lord assist us in the important task.

First, then, the preaching of the gospel. What do we understand by this? Various are the answers given. Some believe it consists of loud declamation and vociferous talking, some in whooping, stamping, and beating the Bible or desk with their fists and in cutting as many odd capers as a wild imagination can suggest; and some err so grievously on this subject as to think that he who hallooes the loudest and speaks the longest is the best preacher. Now all these crude ideas have their origin in our education, for we believe just what we have been taught. But if any man wishes to know what preaching the gospel is, let him not ask of mere mortal man, but let him find his answer in the teachings of Him who spoke and whose wisdom is without mixture of error. Hear Him in the matchless Sermon on the Mount, teaching us to find blessedness in poverty and meekness, in peace and righteousness, in mercy and purity, and to find exceeding great joy in persecution for righteousness' sake. See with what divine skill He expounds the moral law and carries its application beyond the outward and visible conduct into the interior and invisible workings of the human soul. Behold Him either in private houses or on the seashore or in the temple, telling parables of the most striking beauty and simplicity, unfolding the great principles upon which the moral government of the universe is based, enlightening His hearers' understanding and warming their hearts with sunbeams of eternal truth. This is preaching—preaching of the highest kind. We will do well to imitate it, in aid of which let us look for a few moments at the work of the Christian minister as a preacher of the Gospel.

First: It is his business to make man acquainted with his relations to his God as a sinner.

To accomplish this he must re-echo the thunders of Sinai until the slumbering rebel is brought into a sense of his danger and looking into his own heart sees it as a cage of unclean birds or a lair of hissing serpents—the enemy of God by wicked works and the enemy of his own soul. Listening, he hears the fearful silence: "Cursed is every one that continueth not in all things which are written in the book of the law to do them" [Gal. 3:10]. Looking below, he sees hell, as it were, moving from beneath to meet him at his coming; looking above, he beholds an indignant Judge ready to pour out the vials of His wrath upon his guilty and defenseless head. Now hear the cry of his anguished heart: "What shall I do to be saved?" The minister of the gospel answers, "Believe in the Lord Jesus Christ, and thou shalt be saved." Immediately faith springs up

in the soul of this trembling sinner, and looking to Calvary he sees there
the Lamb of God who takes away the sin of the world. With a bounding
heart he exclaims, "My Lord and my God" and feels, pervading his whole
being, a "peace . . . which passeth all understanding" [Phil. 4:7] and "joy
unspeakable and full of glory" [1 Pet. 1:8].

But the work of the gospel minister stops not here: a flock of rich
souls is committed to his care, and it now becomes his duty to train them
for usefulness and for heaven. "But who is sufficient for these things?"

'Tis not a cause of small import
The pastor's care demands;
But what might fill an angel's heart
And filled a Saviour's hands.

Therefore, with all possible diligence he must feed the babes with the
sincere milk of the Word until they are able to eat strong meat. Then he
must feed them with that until they have attained the stature of a man in
Christ Jesus and teach them by all manner of good works to glorify "our
Father who is in heaven." But this does not terminate his work; he must
also, with untiring diligence, arm every soldier of Christ with the panoply
of God and then lead on the sacramental host from truth to truth, from
grace to grace, from victory to victory, until each of them shall have laid
down his armor to take up his crown in heaven. "But who is sufficient
for these things?"

And yet the work of the Christian minister stops not here, for he is to
discipline and govern the church. This brings us to consider:

Second: A very difficult and important part of a minister's duty.

Some of us believe that to discipline the church simply means to
try and expel the incorrigible. Is not this a great mistake? Is it not the
very last thing the pastor should perform? Dear brethren, to discipline
a church implies more than this. It means to indoctrinate, to instruct,
to reprove, to admonish as well as to try and expel. You see, then, what
the pastor's duty is; he is to make his flock intimately acquainted with
the doctrines of the Christian church, instruct them in the principles
of church government, reprove them for negligence and sin, admonish
them concerning their duties and obligations, and then try and expel the
obstinate, so as to keep the church as pure as human wisdom, diligence,

and zeal, under divine guidance, can make it. "But who," I ask, "is sufficient for these things?"

Sufficiency is not to be found in man but in God. Saith the apostle: "Our sufficiency is of God; who also hath made us able ministers of the new testament; not of the letter, but of the spirit; for the letter killeth, but the spirit giveth life" [2 Cor. 3:5-6]. Yes, our sufficiency is of God! But how is this sufficiency to be obtained? Is man a mere passive being in the matter, or does God require some action on his part? We answer, in this respect man is not like a seed placed in the ground that can be developed by the morning and evening dews, together with the native warmth of the earth and sunbeams. He must use the mind that God has given him; he must cultivate this mind and seek the aid that is given to everyone whom he has called to the work of the ministry.

First, then, let him cultivate his mind by all the means in his power. With the light of science, philosophy, and literature, let him illumine his understanding and carry this culture and this illumination to the highest point possible.

Secondly, then, let him seek the unction from above, the baptism of the Holy Ghost. Let him live the life of faith and prayer, the life of unspotted holiness. For such was our Lord and Master, Jesus Christ the Righteous—His head was all knowledge, and His heart all holiness. He was as free from ignorance as He was free from sin. God grant that we may all seek to be like Him as much in the one case as in the other. Then will we be able ministers of the New Testament and will be able with the illustrious Paul to say, "Our sufficiency is of God." Now, it is for teaching sentiments like these that I have been slandered, persecuted, and hated. This has been the head and front of my offending. But, brethren, am I not right? Is it not proper that I should seek the improvement of those who had not the chance for an early education? I have done it, and I still will seek the improvement of all my young brethren, that they may be intelligent, well-educated, and holy men. Like Moses, I can truly say, "Oh, that all the Lord's people were prophets." Yea, indeed, I wish I was the most ignorant man among you, possessing at the same time the amount of information that God has given me, and I deem it very little compared with that which others enjoy.

But to return to the text, I ask, who is sufficient to preach the gospel of Christ and govern the church that he has purchased with his own blood? Who is sufficient to train this host of the Lord and to lead it from earth to heaven? Who is sufficient to guide it through this war against principalities and powers, against spiritual wickedness in high places, against all the hosts of earth and hell, and place it triumphant upon the shining plains of glory? Who is sufficient? I answer, the man who makes Christ the model of his own Christian and ministerial character. This man, and he alone, is sufficient for these things.

The Christian Ministry:
Its Moral and Intellectual
Character (1859)

This sermon was first published in the Repository of Religion and Literature. The journal included the following note: "Bishop Payne's discourse was written at the request of the Literary and Historical Society of the Missouri Conference, read before the Baltimore and Indiana, and the Missouri Conferences, and published by request of the Historical and Literary Societies of the two latter conferences."

The things that thou hast heard of me among many witnesses, the same commit thou unto faithful men, who shall be able to teach others also.
                                        — 2 TIM. 2:2

The teachers of mankind are manifold. There are the teachers of law and of medicine; of mathematics and of language; of natural philosophy, intellectual philosophy, and moral philosophy; of chemistry and botany; of zoology, mineralogy, and geology; of history—natural, secular, and ecclesiastical; of music and of painting.

All these teachers are useful to mankind, and without them the world might ultimately be reduced to barbarism. They are either self-appointed or appointed by men, and they are responsible to men alone for the manner in which they discharge their duties and obligations—they are called professors.

But the teachers of religion and of its highest form, Christianity, are heaven-called, heaven-appointed, heaven-ordained. They are called *ministers* and are responsible first to God, secondarily to man.

It is our intention to consider the character of these latter, morally and intellectually.

I. As to their moral character, the statement of the text is this: they must be *faithful men*.

Now faithfulness in a religious sense, and that is the only sense in which the text uses it, signifies not only *firmness* in our adherence to the truths of religion but also **uprightness** and *integrity* in discharging those duties that religion enjoins upon us.

Let us analyze this thought and see all the elements that enter into its composition. For if we understand the apostle when he uses this word *faithful*, he is only putting a part for the whole—one of the most prominent traits for all the elements of a generic term, including all the graces that constitute the Christian minister's character. He has also furnished the key to this analytic process, for which God be praised. In this, as in everything that man is permitted to touch, man has different standards of measurements, so that what is faithfulness in the estimation of one is not faithfulness in the estimation of another.

Regarding, for example, temperance, one thinks he violates its precepts when he drinks a single glass of wine, another not until he has drank a half dozen glasses, while a third declares than no one is drunk until he has swallowed so much liquor "that he can neither stand nor sit, lie down nor run, in a forty-acre field." So with ministerial faithfulness, men judge differently. Thus a Roman Catholic measures a minister's faithfulness by his implicit obedience to the Popes and the Fathers, a Presbyterian by his scrupulous attachment to the "Confession of Faith," a Baptist by his one-sided view of baptism, a Methodist by his rigid adherence to the discipline of that church, and an Episcopalian by his love for the formula of the *Book of Common Prayer* and the doctrine of apostolic succession.

Then, again, the balance of the scale is affected by the amount of intelligence each of these possesses respecting his distinctive creed, added to the prejudice or candor by which his mind may be colored. Here, then, we see the necessity of perpetual recurrence to the infallible Word of God, for illustration as well as explanation and confirmation of its own doctrines, laws, and precepts.

Doing this we shall find that what is dark in one place may be rendered luminous in another—what is mere statement in this is explanation in that.

Well then, in the text before us the statement is, ministers of Christ must be faithful men. But where is the explanation? My answer is that elements of it are running like veins of gold throughout the epistles of Timothy and Titus and are summed up in the special directions that are given to Timothy for the formation of his own character as a minister in the church of the living God. These are contained in the first epistle, fourth chapter, twelfth verse, and are expressed in the following words: "Let no man despise thy youth; but be thou an example of the believers, in word, in conversation, in charity, in spirit, in faith, in purity."

The moral character of the minister of Jesus, then, must be so elevated that he will be an example of believers:

a. *In his words*. This has reference to his speech both in the pulpit and outside of it. No foolishness, no arrogant sayings, no ludicrous anecdotes, no filthy comparisons, no vulgarity, no obscene epithets, no blasphemous expressions should ever come from his lips—darkening, confusing, disgracing the text that he undertakes to expound. The doctrine, the pure doctrine—the truth, the whole truth, and nothing but the truth—should ever be his utterances, both inside and outside of the pulpit. In the sanctuary and in the parlor, the lips of the righteous must speak wisdom, and his tongue must talk of judgment, so that every word and all his words shall be "like apples of gold in pictures of silver" (Prov. 25:11).

The moral character of the minister of Jesus must be elevated, so he will be an example of the believer.

b. *In conversation*, i.e., in conduct. Oh, how careful should we walk before God and man! Rudeness in behavior disgraces the minister's character, for it lowers the dignity of the Christian ministry. So also does buffoonery, especially pulpit buffoonery, in which some men seem to pride themselves. I have seen some such men whom people fond of fun would just as soon pay twenty-five cents to hear as to see a clown perform in the circus.

Taking liberty with women should be also avoided, as one does a serpent, because a man can no more do this and be sinless than he can put his hands in the fire and escape burning.

Tippling,[11] cigar smoking, and tobacco-chewing are all derogatory to the dignity of a Christian minister. As for drunkenness, what shall I say of the man who is guilty of this? The hog pen suits him much better than the pulpit! Like the adorable Savior in all these respects, he should be a Nazirite. There is not an act that he performs in the presence of others that will be considered apart from his ministerial character.

When a student, I was one day quite languid from excessive study and therefore rose up to take some exercise, but because the weather was inclement, instead of going into the yard for exercise, I began to jump up and down, swinging my arms in a calisthenic manner. At this moment a little boy came into the room to supply me with fuel and not understanding my movements exclaimed, "Preacher dance! preacher dance! Oh, who ever see preacher dance!"

Let us, dear brethren, ever act at home and abroad, in private and in public, as men, conscious that the eyes of God are upon us and that He will hold us responsible for every act, as well as every word, and that He requires us to be as faithful in the former as in the latter. If a man's words can lead others into error, so also his actions may lead them into hell. Moreover, a minister's moral character should be so exalted that he will be an example of the believers.

c. *In charity*, i.e., in love. In this respect his heart should be like a river—not only flowing, but widening and deepening in its onward movements, fertilizing all lands through which it passes, giving drink to every beast of the field and to all the birds of the air, conveying from shore to shore the heaviest and lightest burdens and losing itself not in some quicksand or whirlpool but in the deep ocean of Eternal Love!

To set aside figures and speak plainly, the ministers of Christ should ever have their souls filled with the love of their Master, so that like Him they may endure hunger and thirst, poverty and toils, reproaches and insults, persecution and death. In a word, they must have that love and that degree of it that never shrinks from the cross, giving to their souls the endurance of the ox, the meekness of the lamb, the courage of the lion, the innocence of the dove, the swiftness of the eagle, and the omnipotence of Him whose victory was greatest when He suffered most! Yes, a minister's moral character must be so exalted that he will be an example of the believers.

d. *In spirit*. This idea indicates the sincerity and earnestness of his soul, as well as the meekness, gentleness, and patience in which he performs all his pastoral work and maintains the equilibrium of his character. This gives consistency, strength, and stability to his whole being, subjectively and objectively considered. This makes him like a well-poised column in the sanctuary of the Lord, inclining neither backward nor forward, neither to the right nor the left.

Does he love his God? Yes, not in tongue but in deed, from the depths of his heart. Does he profess love toward the brethren? He means just what he says. Does he engage in the labors of the gospel? He is not a sluggard or an eye-servant but an earnest, diligent laborer who is conscious that although the toil and the pain may be great, yet the reward shall be a thousand times greater. He struggles as though the glorious doctrines of the universe were dependent upon his efforts, and his *alone*. Neither censure nor praise of men can sever his heart from Christ. Pride and ambition, jealousy and malice, hatred and revenge find no nestling place in his heart. Why? Because conscious of his own errors, infirmities, and sins, he casts himself down in the dust and cries, "Unclean! Unclean!" And if at any time he be sensible of doing a virtuous action, his prayer is, "Lord, save me from myself!"

> While I draw this fleeting breath,
> Till my eyes are closed in death,
> When I soar to worlds unknown,
> See Thee on thy judgment throne;
> Rock of Ages, cleft for me,
> Let me hide myself in Thee!

The moral character of the Christian minister must be so elevated that he will be an example of the believers.

e. **In faith**. In this, as in every other quality, he must excel—believing nothing in morals, religion, or doctrine but what God has revealed or what can be proven by His infallible word. Such a man does not turn aside to every humbug or ism that Satan can invent and embrace. Nay, he holds on to the doctrines of the Great Teacher with a strong and steady hand as the only hope for himself and for all!

Such a man will listen to the doctrines and read the Fathers, but he obeys Christ and Christ *alone*, giving reverence to human creeds only so far as they breathe the spirit of the written Word, respecting the Fathers and the doctors only so far as they are echoes of the voice of Christ. Knowing that he has been made one of the stewards of the unsearchable riches of Christ, he will be faithful in faith itself.

But above all, the moral character of the Christian minister must be so exalted that he will be an example of the believers.

f. **In purity**. This virtue includes more than the idea of bodily chastity—it signifies chastity of the spirit, chastity at the very fountainhead of our thoughts, feelings, and actions. It means holiness of the head, heart, and spirit. This must be in the minister a principle as well as a sentiment, a law as well as a purpose.

It is this that makes the Almighty what He really is, not a god but *the God*. For without holiness, He would be nothing more nor less than the greatest devil in the universe. But covering Himself with this as with a garment, and constituting it the beginning and the end of His government, along with all His other infinite attributes, He is the Great God of Moses, glorious in holiness as well as fearful in praises.

We repeat this idea: It is not the magnitude of the sun that constitutes its glory—it is its dazzling light. So also, it is not the omnipotence of God that constitutes His glory—it is His immaculate holiness. And such must be the fact in the moral character of the Christian minister—not his talents, though they be as superior to Newton's as his were superior to the instincts of a brute—not his learning, though that include all that men and angels have ever known—but his holiness.

Drunkenness, fornication, seduction, adultery, together with bigamy and polygamy, must be driven from his heart, as foes alike to God and man. Nor can he make friendship with the men who are guilty of these crimes because he knows that no one can touch filth without having some of it sticking to his finger's end!

What—an adulterer, a fornicator, a seducer, a bigamist in the sanctuary of the Lord as a representative, a minister, of the Lord Jesus Christ? Tell me, has hell a punishment fit for such a wretch?

The minister of Jesus cannot be guilty of such wickedness. He remembers now, and he remembers ever, that the burden of souls is laid upon his heart by the hand that was nailed to the cross—by the hand that burst asunder the bars of death and hell—by the hand that now wields the scepter of the universe—and therefore he cannot betray His trust. No! No! No! He can never do so! He will be faithful even unto death.

Like Job, he eschews evil. Like Paul, his citizenship is in heaven. Like Abraham, he walks before God. Oh, thrice blessed is the estate of such a minister! Treading the earth, his head shall sweep the skies! Dwelling among men, he is even now a citizen of heaven! Great, humble, earnest, holy, faithful man, you are strong in the Lord and in the power of His might. Perhaps your eyes shall not see or your ear hear the ten thousandth part of the good that your faithfulness will effect. Maybe the Great

Redeemer will hide it from you, lest your heart be inflated with spiritual pride, and you fall to rise no more.

Only in the morning of the resurrection shall you behold the works of your hands, the results of your integrity, and then only to fill your soul with wonder, love and praise, causing you to cast your crown of glory at the Redeemer's feet, crying, "Worthy is the Lamb that was slain to receive power, and riches, and wisdom, and strength, and honour, and glory, and blessing" (Rev. 5:12). Verily, verily, you shall *walk* upon the high places of the earth—you shall *stand* upon Mount Zion!

II. We are now prepared to consider the intellectual character of Christian ministers.

The apostle tells us they shall be able to teach others. But may not a man deceive himself on this point? Indeed, he may—many have. There are those who mistake the *desire* to be useful for the *ability*. Now desires and ability are two distinct and independent things. A man may desire to be a king, but this does not qualify him to wield the scepter of a king. So also a man may desire to swim, but if he jumps into a river without the ability, he will soon find himself sinking to the bottom like a stone.

Some men, through mere desire, rush into the ministry without any qualification. They remind me of some lunatics who fancy themselves to be kings or angels and try to act accordingly. I remember such a man who imagined himself a sea captain and did walk up and down the yard with all the air of a commander, ordering one to reef in the main topsails and another to make the soundings.

In like manner some men imagine themselves called to the work of the ministry and desire to engage in it, then obtain a recommendation and license and finally authority from the annual conference. They set out booted, spurred, and mounted, but to do what? You say, to preach the gospel. What gospel? The gospel of Christ? Well, do they? No! They preach what is in no Bible under heaven, not even in the Koran of Mohammed. Rant, obscene language, rude and vulgar expressions, irreverent exclamations, empty-sounding nonsense, and the essence of superstition—these constitute the gospel they preach. By this kind of teaching and this kind of preaching, it has come to pass that some bearing the name of ministers are tipplers and drunkards; others have two living wives, while some laymen have four and yet maintain their standing in the pulpit and in the church. And if you dare to speak of expelling them, others will cry out, "Don't lest you destroy the church."

O, Savior, take care of Your flock! For this reason I "cry aloud" and "spare not." I "lift up [my] voice like a trumpet, and shew my people their transgression, and the house of Jacob their sins" [Isa. 58:1].

For this purpose I say to you, my dear brethren, even if the classes and quarterly conferences let such men deceive them, don't you be deceived by them—let not the Annual Conferences be duped. Nay, let us examine the qualifications of every man who asks admission into the ranks of the ministry; let us try them by the discipline of our church and by the Word of God. To this end let us see what the discipline teaches and what the Word of God commands. Hear the discipline: "Have they gifts as well as graces for the work? Have they, in some tolerable degree, a clear sound understanding, a right judgment in the things of God? A just conception of salvation by faith? And has God given them any degree of utterance? Do they speak readily, justly, clearly?" Such is the distinct, unequivocal declaration of the discipline.

Now hear the Word: "Give attendance to reading, to exhortation, to doctrine. Neglect not the gift that is in thee, which was given thee by prophecy, with the laying on of the hands of the presbytery. Meditate upon these things; give thyself wholly to them; that thy profiting may appear unto all. Take heed unto thyself, and unto the doctrine; continue in them: for in doing this, thou shalt both save thyself, and them that hear thee" (1 Tim. 4:13-16).

Can anyone read this passage without being struck with the nervous language of the apostle? Can anyone hear it without being arrested by its earnestness? Can it be understood without perceiving how the Holy Spirit insists upon a proper and diligent exercise of the intellect for the purpose of improving it by a daily, habitual, continuous contact with the truth, just because truth is the great instrument by which God reveals Himself to man, and by which man is made like unto God?

> *Give attendance to reading. . . . Neglect not the gift that is in thee. . . . Meditate upon these things; give thyself wholly to them, that thy profiting may appear to all.*

All these expressions show the solicitude of the Eternal Spirit and the deepness of the impression Paul desired to make upon the mind of

Timothy, causing him to feel and know that he was not to be a mere drone in the hive, a snail in the garden, or a lounger about the house of God, but that he had a mind, and that mind was made for thinking, investigating, discriminating—for study.

Therefore, neglect would lead to disastrous consequences. The Christian minister has no more liberty to cease from the cultivation of his mind than the ocean has to cease its motion. Think of the disastrous consequences of the latter, and you will see the consequences of the former. If the ocean ceased to move, its waters would become as stagnant as those of a rain barrel. Every fish in it would perish, the whole atmosphere would be pregnant with pestilence, and the green earth itself would be struck with universal palsy and become a field of graves!

So also with the ministers of Jesus. If they cease to cultivate their minds by the study of holy truth, they will retrograde back to the darkness, superstition, and errors of heathenism, religion would become a mere cloak of hypocrisy, with blasphemy the language of its teachers, and the church itself, like the temple at Jerusalem, would once more hear the awful words, "Let us depart, let us depart."

What, then, is the just inference that enlightened reason draws from the text when it commands not only Timothy but all the presbyters, elders, and bishops in all countries throughout all ages, "The things which thou hast heard of me among many witnesses, the same commit unto faithful men, who shall be able to teach others also" (2 Tim. 2:2). It teaches us that we are bound to entrust the unsearchable riches of Christ only to men who have:

a. *Improvable minds*—that is, minds capable of cultivation. This lies at the foundation of all ministerial usefulness. It is like the gold in the crude and flinty quartz that needs to pass through the crucible in order that its intrinsic excellence may be made manifest, or the rude marble in the quarry that passes through the creative hands of the sculptor in order that it may be transformed into a beautiful statute of living, active, glorious manhood.

But it is not enough that a man possess an improvable mind—he must also have:

b. *An unquenchable desire for useful knowledge.*

Without the latter, the former is like a locomotive without steam—nothing but useless machinery. But if this desire is so strong that the person is content as long as he is acquiring knowledge, then this man has in his nature another element of ability to teach others.

c. *He must also have application.* This is essential, for if he has it not, his reading will be as seldom as it will be desultory. He will be ever learning, yet never coming to the knowledge of the truth—ever swimming on the surface, but never descending through the clear, deep waters to the gemmed bottom of the Ocean of Sciences, nor rising through sublime heights of Christian philosophy to the luminous temple of revelation and there make his dwelling among the angels of God.

Brother, you can know whether you possess this essential quality by looking at the manner in which you have pursued your studies. If you read today and neglect it tomorrow, if you study this month and omit the next, then you will never be able to teach others the deep things of the Spirit of Truth because you yourself will never reach them. What a man does not have, he can never give to others.

Permit me to assure you, dear brother, that deep, clear, and solid learning is not—cannot—be attained by the reading of a few hours, a few months, or a few years but is the result of a life devoted to patient, diligent, and careful study of truth in all its ramifications and in all its relations.

The men to whom we commit the unsearchable riches of Christ must also:

d. Be men of *correct judgment.*

Those who teach immortal souls must have this great qualification. And inasmuch as it involves the power of comparison, it will enable him to discern the resemblance and dissimilarity between one doctrine and another, to discriminate between falsehood and truth, to scrutinize the opinions, conduct, and character of men, and also to trace the eternal distinctions that a wise, just, and good Creator has established between right and wrong, between good and evil, between virtue and vice.

It will also teach him how to adapt the different truths of the gospel to the varying condition and character of the children of men. For Paul does not preach at Athens all the same truths that he uttered at Jerusalem; and also his Epistle to the Hebrews differs very much from that which he addressed to the Romans.

Moreover, a correct judgment will give him the ability to hold the reins of ecclesiastical government with such a hand and to execute it in such a spirit as will save him from timidity on the one hand and rashness on the other. And therefore in him human passions shall neither hush the voice of Justice nor silence the pleadings of Mercy. Rather these Godlike attributes shall cheerfully embrace and sweetly kiss each other when the claims of the former shall have been met by the proffers and sacrifices of the latter.

Moreover, the unsearchable riches of the gospel must be committed only to men:

e. Who have a *natural aptness to teach others*. This is a rare qualification, as great as it is rare, and imposes upon him who possesses it a tremendous yet glorious responsibility. It is to him in whom it dwells what light is to the sun, so that while he is himself covered with this glorious element, he is shedding the same blessing upon all around him.

It is his pleasure, his happiness, to teach others, and he cannot do otherwise. He can no more keep from teaching others than the sun can refuse to shine upon all; and like the sun, he often does it when he is not even conscious of it.

The end of all his studies and research into religion, science, and philosophy is to teach immortal souls and lead them to the knowledge of the truth as it is in Christ Jesus. He does not mistake sound for sense, any more than he could mistake stones for bread, giving the people the former just because he has not the latter. He is more anxious to make God's people intelligent and wise than to excite their animal feelings and make them shout. He labors not to make them admire and praise himself but to make them angry with themselves, fall out with their sins, and fall in love with Christ. And this he does by all plainness of speech and fitness of simile, by arguments as strong as bars of iron, by illustrations as beautiful as the lily and the rose.

Having these five, there is one other qualification that he must not fail to possess:

f. *It is humility*. This is partly intellectual and partly moral. It is intellectual inasmuch as its root is a knowledge of one's self or one's ability, one's character. It is moral inasmuch as it is a deep sense of one's own unworthiness and comparative insignificance as a man, a scholar, and a Christian.

So humility, instead of being incompatible with a knowledge of one's own self, is the result of that knowledge. This is the convincing or conservative principle among the graces. It is to them what salt is to meat. Without humility, talents and learning are but the accomplishments of a devil. Without humility, faith, love, and holiness are evanescent graces that will cower and perish in the presence of the tempter.

This is the grace that keeps the souls down, down, down in the dust, at the very foot of the cross, causing a man to look upon himself as nothing and upon Christ as all.

Oh, how sensitive is this man about his Master's honor! How solicitous for his Master's glory! How tremblingly alive to his own ignorance, his own weakness, his utter insufficiency! From the depths of his soul he is ever crying, *Lord, Thou knowest my weakness—be Thou my strength. Thou knowest my ignorance—be Thou my wisdom. Teach me, that I may not be a blind leader of the blind, but a scribe well instructed unto the Kingdom of Heaven. Oh, let not the people see me; let them see You in Your vesture dipped in blood. Let them not hear me; let them hear You in Your voice of saving truth!* Like the beloved John, this man's greatest ambition is to lean his head upon the bosom of Jesus and catch the lessons of unerring wisdom as they fall from His sacred lips, and therefore he is able to teach others.

Like David, he is ever conversing with nature; like Paul, he is the great student of revelation. Therefore, like both he is able to teach others.

To sum up all our ideas in a single sentence, he must be holy, studious, instructive, and wise, ever keeping his heart in contact with the Spirit of God, ever drinking from the pure fountains of truth. He teaches himself, that he may be able to teach others also.

To such a man, the Pauline injunction comes with heavenly emphasis and power: "Thou, therefore, my son, be strong in the grace that is in Christ Jesus."

The blacksmith must have strong muscles to wield the sledgehammer, and the soldier the broad sword. The minister of the Lord Jesus has to contend with principalities and powers, with spiritual wickedness in high places, and so he above all men must be strong in the grace that is in Christ Jesus.

Let the same principle of incorruptible holiness, divine life, and self-sacrifice that caused the Great Teacher to go about doing good also be in you. Let this principle be in your soul, invigorating and imparting to you the strength of an angel, causing you to fly about doing good, and nothing but good.

In conclusion, brethren, what now is our duty? To whom shall we commit the unsearchable riches of Christ? To drunkards, bigamists, and polygamists? To drones and loungers? To men having "skulls that will not learn and cannot teach"? God forbid! Rather let us die than commit such a crime against God and man. Oh, let that other command of the apostle to Timothy be ever sounding in our ears: "Lay hands suddenly upon no man, neither be partaker of other men's sins: keep thyself pure" [1 Tim. 5:22]. Yes, let each one of us understand this mandate and know and feel that any man who enters the ministry without the proper qualifications, moral and intellectual, which are indicated by the text, sins against God; and he who helps such a man to get into the ministry also sins against Him.

Whenever a young man comes forward and tells us that he is called to the ministry, let us examine him rigidly, according to our excellent discipline and the requisitions of God's Word. It is not enough that he tells us God has called him; let him show the evidences of his call. Some of us are too credulous. If a man tells us that he is called to this work, we believe without proof; without any qualification, we are ready to push him into the sacred office. His say so is not enough.

Do you not know that "fools rush in where angels fear to tread"? He who aids a man in committing murder is himself guilty of it. This is true in the State, and it is no less so in the church. This has often been done. Some men have no conscience, regard no vows, care for no responsibility that they assume, and discharge no obligation that they take upon themselves. They will *destroy* a sheep as soon as they will *save* one.

Let us consider our Lord and Master, that great Shepherd of the sheep, whom an inspired apostle calls the Chief Shepherd. Let us study His character, examine His matter and His manner, and fashion ourselves according to His lofty model. As a man, He had all these qualifications and more. We do not say that all ministers can have them in the same degree. But this we do maintain, that he who has them in the largest possible degree will be the most successful teacher, preacher, and shepherd.

Some men have gifts but no graces. Others have graces but no gifts. Neither of these are wanted in the Christian ministry. "I charge thee before God, and the Lord Jesus Christ, and the elect angels, that thou observe these things without preferring one before another, doing nothing by partiality" (1 Tim. 5:21).

Labor diligently to purify your own hearts from sin, to enrich your own minds with every kind of useful knowledge, to be clothed with humility as with a garment, and thus to be qualified to teach others also.

On the Committee of Examination, recommend no man who is not able to teach others. In your quarterly conferences, so far as you have power, suffer no man to obtain a license who is not able to teach others.

Will you dare vote for a man to obtain ordination who is not able to teach others? No, never! Let the whole ministry, let the whole church, pray that the Lord Jesus may give us ministers full of holiness, wisdom, and faithfulness "who shall be able to teach others also." Amen and amen! *Lord Jesus, let it be now and forever.*

The Divinely Approved Workman:
Semi-Centennial Sermon (1874)

The General Conference of 1872 was a disappointment to Payne, as he observed "many things said and done . . . inconsistent with the Christian spirit." The conference, according to Payne, was filled with the worst sort of politics. With the death of long-time bishop William P. Quinn in 1873 and financial trouble at Wilberforce, perhaps this address is best understood as an attempt to set down a more full summary of his views on education and the ministry as he approached retirement. This sermon was delivered in February 1874 at Allen Chapel AME in Cincinnati, Ohio.

> *Study to shew thyself approved unto God, a workman that needeth not to be ashamed, rightly dividing the word of truth. . . . And the servant of the Lord must not strive; but be gentle unto all men, apt to teach, patient, in meekness instructing those that oppose themselves; if God peradventure will give them repentance to the acknowledging of the truth.*
>
> —2 TIMOTHY 2:15, 24-25.

The word *workman* implies work to be done and a master to oversee the work that is to be done. It also implies a house, an edifice, a temple—more or less important, more or less grand, more or less durable, lasting for centuries, accommodating generation after generation. This supposition covers the facts of the case to be considered because the church of God is called "the house of God" [1 Tim. 3:15], a "holy temple" [Eph. 2:21], "the temple of the living God" [2 Cor. 6:16]. But this temple is a spiritual temple. The workman, therefore, must do spiritual work in this spiritual temple; and his work is all the while under the sleepless eye of the Omniscient Master, who is solicitous about the manner as well as the ability of the workman, because this temple is of the highest importance as well as of vast dimensions and durability embracing all time and all races and therefore all the generation of men.

Now each local church is nothing more and nothing less than a chamber in this Spiritual Temple, and the Divine Master is equally interested in its purity, perfection, and beauty. But to do this the workman should study the character of his Master as well as the work that is to be done. And this leads us to the first thing in the text that is to be expounded—the question, what is to be studied? First, he must study God in order that he may learn the character of the Master whom he has to serve and conform his own character to that Master's will. Now God has manifested and is manifesting Himself in three different ways. The workman, therefore, will do well to study these manifestations of the Deity.

a. The first is *Nature* around us. We cannot open our eyes or ears without seeing forms and hearing voices speaking in behalf of an existing but invisible Deity. In these we shall find proofs of His wisdom, power, and goodness and recognize the fact that these attributes are infinite.

b. In *history* we also have manifestations of God. We see these in the origin, progress, and complete development of a nation's greatness with its decline, old age, and death, in which we see exhibitions of the retributive justice and providence of God as the Almighty Ruler of races and nations, kingdoms and empires. We see God humbling the arrogant pride of despots, as in the case of Nebuchadnezzar; exalting the humble and the wise, as in the case of Daniel; punishing crime, as in the case of David and rewarding incorruptible virtue, as in the person of Joseph; breaking the arm of the brazen-hearted and blasphemous enslaver, as he did that of Pharaoh; and out of an enslaved race producing a great people, as illustrated by the history of the Israelites. Nor does God manifest Himself in the history of races, nations, and governments only. He does this also in that kind of personal history that we call biography. No one—that is, no thinking mind—can read the biography of Joseph or Job, of Abraham or Jacob among the Patriarchs, or of Luther and Wesley among the Reformers, without discovering an invisible, supernatural power behind and above these men, inspiring, guiding, and protecting them, planning their plans and executing their victories. All this is attributable to none other than the omniscient, almighty, beneficent Being whom we recognize as God and whom we are ever inclined to call the God of Abraham, Isaac, and Jacob.

c. But above all these there is *revelation*, in which the infinite has manifested Himself as He has done nowhere else. In physical nature we see exhibitions of His infinite wisdom, power, and goodness. In history we have evidences of His inflexible justice and beneficent providence, as well as his unquestionable sovereignty. But in revelation we see His mercy moving hand in hand with His justice, His unutterable love hand in hand with His immaculate holiness, and all these directed and controlled by His unerring wisdom, constraining the philosophic mind to exclaim, "O the depth of the riches both of the wisdom and knowledge of God! how unsearchable are his judgments, and his ways past finding out" (Rom. 11:33).

Now when the studious workman has prosecuted such studies and made such researches as we have indicated, he will feel the necessity of unceasing efforts to secure the approbation of God, from whom he professes to have received a commission to preach the gospel, and consequently of so conducting himself in the presence of his omniscient Master that he may never have cause to be ashamed.

But of what may this workman be ashamed? Of two things: his ignorance and his vices. So varied and so deep are the truths with which the Christian minister has to deal that unless he is a careful, prayerful, and diligent student of that one book, the Bible, he will often be compelled to blush at his ignorance. And let this workman know that to understand that as it ought to be understood and to apply its varied important teachings as they ought to be applied, it is necessary that he make himself master of many other books.

Revelation is the field above all others that the Christian workman must study, in order that he may become acquainted with the ineffable character of his Lord and Master, for there he will find the truth that so august a Sovereign demands a servant of no contemptible character. The dignity and kindness of this Master will impress themselves so deeply upon his understanding and his affections that he will be disposed to conform his own character to that of his Master.

The slaves of educated and opulent masters in South Carolina always felt themselves as having a standing and character better than the slaves of ignorant and poverty-stricken masters. So also the ambassador of a great and powerful empire feels a dignity and importance that he who represents a state with small resources and feeble power cannot possibly feel. Now what is true of such servants ought to be far more true of the man who represents the King of kings and Lord of lords.

But there is another source of knowledge concerning the Deity that this workman must also study. It is man in his threefold nature—physical, mental, and moral—his spiritual nature. In these he will find a manifestation of wisdom, skill, power, and goodness, which at once demonstrates the character of the Master whom he serves.

A study of the mental nature of man will increase the evidence of the almightiness and infinite wisdom of his Master, and an acquaintance with his moral nature will serve to give him still greater evidences of the glorious character of the Infinite. The spiritual nature of his being is the crystallization of his moral nature, as his moral nature is the sublimation of his mental. In him you will see a wonderful blending of weakness and strength, of good and evil—the qualities of a devil alternating with those of an angel, the attributes of a worm blending with those of a god. In him you will find the heart that weeps and bleeds, that hopes and fears, that hates and loves, that crawls in the dust and wings its flight toward heaven. In him you shall see the will now moving backward with the stubbornness of a mule and then onward with the alacrity of a seraph. So in the study of man the Christian workman will find the answer to the question of the inspired poet: "What is man, that thou art mindful of him? and the son of man, that thou visitest him?" (Ps. 8:4; Heb. 2:6).

Oh, there is such a length and breadth, such a height and depth, such variety and richness, such beauty and sublimity, such joy in these studies, in these researches, that the intelligent workman, who is anxious to secure the divine approbation, will have no time for mere amusements, gossip, or indolence.

Let this workman so study that he shall not have occasion to be ashamed of his ignorance. But the Christian workman may also be ashamed of a vice contracted in his previous life, which is called the besetting sin. Let the workman beware of this evil against which there is no shield but the refuge of the Savior's wings. There the believer is safe; from the grasp of our Lord's omnipotent hand no power can pluck him. But this implies holy living—not sinlessness but eternal vigilance against sin, persistent opposition to temptation. And where resistance itself might result in defeat, one must find safety in flight; but the refuge to which he flies is none other than that of the Almighty wings.

We are to love all men so that we shall always be devising and planning for their well-being, including even the man whom we may partly regard as an enemy. Love to all will make us do justice to all; and a man who thus loves will always find himself at one with the Judge of all the Earth, and therefore approved by Him. This love is sometimes called godliness. Of this manner of life, this kind of moral conduct, a workman shall never have occasion to be ashamed.

Moreover, this workman must not strive; he must not be contentious, quarrelsome, threatening those who oppose him with personal violence, treating as enemies all who differ from him in opinion, principles, or measures. Rather he must patiently instruct those who oppose him. Some men cannot see the right, the true, or the good. Men who oppose these things are actually opposed to themselves. It is right to meekly teach the opposers of the truth in order that God may grant them repentance and cause them to obey and defend that which they have been so ready to oppose. Such must be the workmen who may fill this pulpit in the future. They will be needed to lead the future interests of this church.

And now it is time that we should review the history of this local church of the Church Militant, in order that we may see what it has accomplished and learn what it may and must do for future conquests in behalf of God and man. Besides the development and establishment of itself, from a very small and weak beginning into a numerous and powerful society, it has planted a small and at present a weak congregation on Walnut Hills. Is this work enough for half a century? I think not. I think it ought to have accomplished more than this. I feel certain that if its membership had been alive to the work of Christ, more could have been accomplished. Instead of one powerful church, we might have had three or four. "He which soweth sparingly shall reap also sparingly" [2 Cor. 9:6]. "As thou hast believed, so be it done unto thee" [Matt. 8:13; 15:28]. Again, what has this church done for Christian education? Our dear Brother Arnett tells us that of twenty-one colored teachers now employed in the colored schools of Cincinnati, nine are members of our two churches or are attached to them—i.e., they professedly worship in them. This is a handsome proportion because, besides ours, there are six other churches. But did Allen Temple educate these nine teachers by direct efforts put forth on her part? Let the officers of Allen Temple answer.

Again, did Allen Temple ever send a young man to Wilberforce to prepare himself for the work of the Christian ministry, and having sent one there, did she ever support him until his educational course was completed? If you have enjoyed the ministry of men wholly or partially educated, was it or was it not because they were forced upon you by circumstances beyond your control, or was it by your direct agency? Is it not generally true that our progress in an educational direction may be likened to that which the freight trains make along the railroad? But if this has been the case in the past, it ought not be so in the future. We ought to put forth systematic and direct efforts for our own progress in all that is good and useful. As a denomination we have done well in planning and building churches during the last half century; let us now go to work to plan and build schools of learning. Let this church plan for and systematically educate her young men for the ministry. Let the official board lead the way by planning the work, and I am certain the people—i.e., the members of this church—will sustain them in their efforts. So at the end of every five or six years this church can send out a young man well prepared to be a workman approved unto God.

There are also your daughters. They ought to be the objects of your special regard. To educate them in such a manner as to render them fit to do Christian work is the highest duty of the church herself. She can perform none higher, none more beneficial for the community. And whenever a young woman of talents and piety is found, who has aptness for teaching and who is desirous to qualify herself thoroughly for such a work but has not the means to meet the expenses, this church ought to undertake to educate her. Perhaps there is no greater power in a given community than that of educated women. I use the term in its broadest, highest sense, by which I do not mean a smattering, or even excellence in music, instrumental and vocal, in drawing and painting; nor do I mean a mere classical or scientific and mathematical training. But I do mean a Christian education, that which draws our head and heart toward the Cross, and after consecrating them to the Cross sends the individuals from beneath the Cross with the spirit of Him who died upon it, sending them abroad well fitted for Christian usefulness, a moral, a spiritual power, molding and coloring the community, and preparing it for a nobler and higher state of existence in that world where change never comes, unless it be a change from the good to the better and from the better to the best.

The past, the dark past, is gone—I hope forever gone. It was the time when ignorance sat in high places and ruled, when vice was as much respected as virtue. The present and the future demands a different spirit and different conduct. The almighty fiat is gone forth. "Many shall run to and fro, and knowledge shall be increased" (Dan. 12:4). Hence the future demands educated women in order that there may be educated wives, and consequently educated mothers who will give to the race a training entirely and essentially different from the past. In other words, the future demands wives and mothers who will, like Susannah Wesley, convert the homestead into a schoolhouse, and that schoolhouse into a church where young immortals shall be trained for their heavenward flight. The wants of the race demand such women to descend into the South as educators, to assist in correcting the religious errors of the freedmen and to bridle their wild enthusiasm. These religious errors, the wild enthusiasm of the freedmen, are results of the slavery that had been operating upon them and their forefathers for nearly 250 years and cannot be removed in a day, nor by one man, nor by one kind of human agency. The Deity does not operate upon humanity in that fashion. He applies a multitude of instrumentalities and different agencies to civilize and Christianize a race, among which are the educators of a race. But of these none are more potent than the educated wife, the educated mother, the educated school-mistress, but educated under the Cross and in the spirit of Him who died upon the cross.

There is also the work of Christian missions at home and abroad. A careful and impartial review of the history of Allen Temple shows that in this direction that church had done but little. This sturdy tree during the past fifty years should have sent its roots **under** the Ohio if it could not send them across it; and by this time there should have been at least two young trees vigorously flowering and fruiting on the soil of Kentucky. But we have said, let the past errors and blunders be buried with the past. At the same time let us study the fact that a new leaf with its pages has been added to the volume of our history. But let us not study this fact alone; let us go beyond that to the philosophy that lies behind and beneath it. In so doing, we will learn the great lesson that history teaches. That lesson is this: every revolution that passes over a nation evolves principles that while they appear new are really as old as humanity and were involved in its very nature at its conception in the mind of the Creator. These principles give birth to new sentiments, new laws, new customs, which the church of God must consider and take into account in all her subsequent operations. The denomination that will not take these changes into consideration and act accordingly must become extinct.

Progressive humanity, led on by the hand of its Omnipotent Father, will leave it behind like a ship on a sandbar or throw it out as salt that has lost its savor. In either case the extinction of such a denomination or such a local society of Christians is as certain as the extinction of the Jewish church. Christianity is an educating power. It educates in every direction that touches humanity—not religiously only, but morally also; not morally only, but intellectually also; and not intellectually only. Because it is a religious, moral, and intellectual educational power, it logically affects and modifies all forms of civil and political life.

Now the important question that Allen Temple has to consider and determine is: will she become an educating and missionary power as Christ Jesus designs her to be or will she refuse? There are two negative ways in which she may answer this question—the one by a direct no and the other by pleading poverty. Either of these answers will prove fatal to her influence, prosperity, and perpetuity. Therefore, the only wise answer she can give is, "Lo, I come to do thy will, O God!" To be willing to do is to get the power to do. Let Allen Temple resolve to educate and to assist in spreading the Redeemer's kingdom from pole to pole. Then let her immediately execute this resolution by organized, systematic, and persistent efforts, and the means will be supplied by Him who has said, "Ask, and it shall be given you; seek, and ye shall find" (Matt. 7:7).

Let Allen Temple take this advice, which is calmly and considerately given, and she will make a grand, a glorious history during the next fifty years. To educate the immortal mind and prepare it for eminent usefulness on earth and the unutterable glory of heaven, to assist in transforming this dark earth into "the Holy City—the New Jerusalem," is a work in which the cherubim and seraphim would be happy to labor. Oh, that God would give to Allen Temple a missionary and an educating spirit, the mind that was in Jesus Christ.

PART THREE

Francis J. Grimké:

The Gospel and the Church in the World

The history of slave and master in the American South is a complicated one, involving brutalities and intimacies equal in their intensity and in their impact on all concerned. One such instance is the life of Francis James Grimké (1850–1937). Born October 10, 1850 to a slave mother, Nancy Weston, and her owner, Henry Grimké, he was the son of an aristocratic slaveholding family in Charleston, South Carolina and a relative of the famous abolitionist sisters Angelina and Sarah Moore Grimké. After the death of his wife in 1843 Henry Grimké found in Nancy Weston a suitable "wife" and mother for three children—Archibald Henry, Francis James, and John.[1]

Henry Grimké died of yellow fever when Francis was five years old, having stipulated that Nancy Weston and all of her children be placed in the possession of his oldest son and Francis's half-brother, E. Montague. By custom, Montague was to "retain nominal ownership" and "regard the slaves as members of the family, thereby insuring their virtual freedom."[2] Montague respected the informal freedom intended by Henry Grimké for five years before attempting to re-enslave the three boys to personally serve his second wife. Francis attempted to avoid being re-enslaved by joining the Confederate Army, where he served for two years as an officer's valet. Young Francis managed to evade Montague's plots until Emancipation. After Emancipation, Mrs. Frances Pillsbury, the administrator of Morris Street School and a veteran educator and abolitionist from the north, sent Francis and his brother Archibald to Massachusetts to continue their education.

While in Massachusetts, Grimké worked in a shoe factory and resided temporarily in the barn of a Dr. John Brown of Stoneham, Massachusetts. It was there that he also developed an interest in medicine. Later the South Carolina school administrator and his aunts, Sarah and Angelina Grimké, made arrangements for him to move to Chester County, Pennsylvania to study medicine at recently renamed Lincoln University. Grimké distinguished himself as a scholar at Lincoln, graduating in 1870 as class valedictorian. In 1871 he began studying law at Lincoln, and in 1872 he moved to Washington, D.C. to continue pursuit of a law degree at Howard University.

Princeton theologian and seminary president Charles Hodge (1797–1878).
Francis Grimké studied with Hodge from 1874 to 1878.

While at Howard University, Grimké felt called to the Christian ministry. He left Howard in 1874 to pursue theological education at Princeton Theological Seminary under the leadership of Charles Hodge. At Princeton, Francis received a thoroughly Reformed understanding of the Christian faith grounded in a high view of the inspiration, inerrancy, and authority of the Scriptures. In 1936, sixty-two years after his entrance to Princeton, he wrote in his journal:

I accept, and accept without reservation, the Scriptures of the Old and New Testaments as God's Word, sent to Adam's sinful race and pointing out the only way by which it can be saved. [W]ithout the Holy Scriptures and what they reveal, there is no hope for humanity. To build on anything else is to build on the sand.[3]

Grimké graduated from Princeton in 1878 and soon after began his public ministry at the affluent 15th Street Presbyterian Church in Washington, D.C. On December 19 of that same year Grimké married Charlotte Forten, granddaughter of influential businessman, activist, and abolitionist James Forten, Sr. of Philadelphia. Charlotte inherited her grandfather's—indeed the Forten family's—activist character and along with Francis formed a formidable duo for racial justice and women's rights. At the time of their marriage Charlotte was forty-one and Francis twenty-eight. The couple gave birth to one daughter in June 1880, but the child died in infancy.

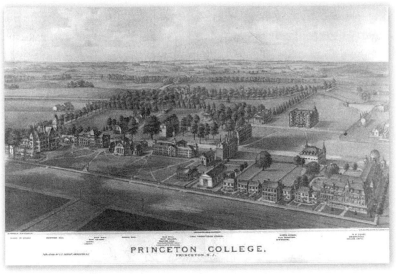

PRINCETON COLLEGE.
PRINCETON, N.J.

Princeton College, Princeton, New Jersey in 1875. Grimké attended
Princeton Seminary from 1874 to 1878, earning a Doctorate of Divinity degree.

Aside from a brief stint from 1885–1889 at Laura Street Church in Jacksonville, Florida, Grimké served as pastor of 15th Street Presbyterian Church for his entire six decades of Christian ministry. He declined offers to teach at Biddle University and the presidency of Howard University, choosing instead a life of shepherding God's people. But in no sense was choosing the pastorate a withdrawal from the world. Perhaps one of the greatest lessons one can glean from Francis Grimké's life is his tenacious insistence on both the primacy of the gospel preaching ministry and the need for fully engaging the affairs of the world. The centrality of the preached Word he learned from an early mentor, Dr. John B. Reeve, a graduate of Columbia University and Union Theological Seminary and pastor of Philadelphia's Central Church.[4] Grimké's hard-won victory over injustice supplied a tenacity for tackling the difficulties of the world. In the history of the Christian church, most men have been swept to one or another extreme of this tension—preferring either a full embrace of the world to the detriment of the gospel ministry or retreating into "Christian" seclusion and absconding from the affairs of the world. Dr. Francis Grimké offers a case study in how to hold this tension without being torn in two.

Dr. Grimké's pastoral career spanned the tumultuous periods from Reconstruction through the post-World War I era. The social changes and upheavals accompanying these periods, Grimké believed, required the guidance of men and women tutored by the gospel of Jesus Christ and fortified with Christian character. Though he remained first and foremost a pastor, Christian engagement with public pursuits was critical. A significant portion of his life was dedicated to wider public aims—serving as a trustee at Howard University, helping found the National Association for the Advancement of Colored People (NAACP) in 1906, creating educational opportunities, improving race relations, and encouraging suffrage.

And nowhere was his public life more critical and stinging than in his appraisal of the church and "Christian" hypocrisy in the face of injustice.

> He thought of men and measures as good or bad. Expediency did not figure very much in his make-up. Diplomacy did not count for much with him. What could not be justified as the proper thing for mankind he frankly disapproved. His creed was to do right and thus be in a position to urge upon others the same duty without fear and trembling. He never preached what he did not earnestly try to practice. For the hypocrite he had the greatest contempt. He had no use for the minister

who selfishly advanced himself at the expense of the church, or who used the pulpit to advertise himself before the world.[5]

From his own upbringing, Grimké knew the contradiction between profession and committed action. He witnessed the lash applied to enslaved Africans and the inhumane cruelty of selling "brothers" to the highest bidder. That the particular band of "brothers" known as Christians could be capable of the same treacherous hypocrisy was plain to Grimké as he observed the silence and inaction of both white and black churches in the face of racial injustice. Consequently he dedicated himself to exposing the role of the church in the world. Even after Charlotte's death in 1914, when Francis grew more introspective and reflective and eventually resigned from his pastoral responsibilities, he continued to write, journal, and comment on the state of the church and the ministry. Grimké died on October 11, 1937 in Washington, D.C.

He understood that two great obstacles assaulted the church: ignorance and demagogism. Ignorance he thought could be combated with education and learning. But demagogism, or "the combination of unprincipled men within the church to get control, the monopoly of all positions of honor and trust of a general character," needed the warring reaction of godly men who would protect the church and drive out unprincipled men. Without such a warfare, Francis Grimké believed, "the usefulness of the church [was] at an end," and though "it may increase in numbers . . . in moral and spiritual power it will become a constantly diminishing factor."[6]

No stronger charge and warning could be issued to today's pastors and church leaders. In our time we need to hear the voice of Dr. Francis James Grimké as he beckons us to *both* reform the church and the men who lead her and to reform society with the gospel of Jesus Christ and Christian witness.

The sermons and addresses of Francis Grimké included in this volume represent a brief sampling of his messages aimed at chiding the church—black and white—into more aggressive and righteous stances against injustices. They illustrate his concern for reforming the church, for encouraging her toward greater integrity and accepting responsibility for being salt and light in the world. Grimké fought hard to maintain a gospel focus in all his ministerial endeavors and to apply that focus to the major social issues of his day. It seems to have always been the case that pastors are asked to represent every social concern their congregations and communities deem important. Grimké offers us one model for preserving and emphasizing the primary calling of preaching the gospel with Christ-centered activism in important social concerns.

In his 1892 sermon "The Afro-American Pulpit in Relation to Race Elevation," Grimké sets his gaze on the issue of race elevation or progress among African-Americans and the responsibility that the African-American church owned in that progress. Grimké's thesis was, "If we [African-Americans] are to stand, if our rise is to be permanent, if we are not to pass away like the morning mist, or wither like the grass, beneath the material and intellectual there must be a moral basis." For Grimké, the essential ingredient to progress was character, Christian character. "What we need most of all is character," he declared in the opening lines. In "The Afro-American Pulpit in Relation to Race Elevation," he sought to raise up a biblical standard for ministers in their endeavor to build character and to evaluate whether his contemporaries were in fact meeting that standard. Ministers, he argued, were to follow the examples provided by the prophets, the apostles, and most importantly Christ Jesus Himself. The standard that Jesus and His messengers raised was faithfulness in proclaiming justification by faith alone in Christ alone on the one hand and the outworking of that faith in Christian virtue as evidence of genuine faith on the other. Grimké maintained that if a minister were to "fulfill his high mission as God's representative and . . . make himself felt as a moral force in properly directing the budding and expanding life about him," he must both faithfully proclaim the gospel and also faithfully cultivate Christian character in himself and his people.

Against this backdrop, Grimké offered a scathing evaluation of the African-American pulpit of his day and a prescient description of many pulpits in our own day. Dr. Grimké concluded that while there were certainly faithful and gifted men serving in African-American churches, emotionalism, levity or frivolity, and greed characterized too many pulpits. These three factors, according to Grimké, produced disastrous results on both the church and ultimately on society. Emotionalism yielded little or no biblical instruction for the people, required no serious study from the preacher, lowered the spiritual state of the congregation, and defiled the very idea of biblical religion. Levity and frivolity destroyed the solemnity of worship and rendered "the House of God in many cases . . . a mere playhouse for the entertainment and amusement of the people." And according to Grimké, greed for money caused the church to degenerate into "a mere agency for begging." If the church were to play her part in the advancement of African-American families and communities, she needed to solve the problem of giving to the people not what they found most congenial but what was "most effective in developing in them a true manhood and womanhood, in making them good fathers and mothers, good husbands and wives, good citizens and neighbors," the kind of preaching that yields "the largest returns in purity, in honesty, in sobriety, in sweetness, in gentleness." This is the kind of preaching and ministry we need today as well.

If "The Afro-American Pulpit and Its Relation to Race Elevation" chastised black pastors who were performing beneath the high call of Christian ministry, "Christianity and Race Prejudice" excoriated the white Christian church for its duplicity in race-related problems. Dr. Grimké chose for his text the famous exchange between Jesus and the Samaritan woman at the well in John 4:9—"How is it that thou, being a Jew, askest drink of me, which am a woman of Samaria? for the Jews have no dealings with the Samaritans." The first part of the sermon, delivered on May 29, 1910, presented a basic description of race prejudice, the tenets of Christianity, and an exploration of the attitude of American Christianity toward race prejudice. Grimké held race prejudice to be utterly contradictory to the character of Jesus and the principles of Christianity—"there is not to be found anywhere in the religion of Jesus Christ anything upon which it can stand, anything by which it can be justified, or even extenuated."

In the second part of the sermon, delivered on June 5, 1910 and reprinted in this volume, Grimké inspected the attitude of the white church as a visible, local institution toward race prejudice. He proclaimed that race prejudice was in almost absolute control of the practice of churches, congregations, and professing Christians. He lamented the very existence of such a thing as "white churches" and "black churches," asking:

> Why should there be churches made up of white Christians, and churches made up of colored Christians in the same community, and, where all speak the same language; why should white Christians and colored Christians not feel perfectly at home with each other in the same religious gatherings, if they are all Christians, if they all believe in

the Fatherhood of God, and the brotherhood of man, in doing by others as they would be done by, in loving each other as they love themselves, in their oneness in Christ Jesus, and if the same Holy Spirit dwells alike in all their hearts?

Grimké confessed to being surprised at "how little influence the religion of Jesus Christ has had in controlling the prejudice of men, in lifting them above the low plane upon which race prejudice places them." He found professing Christians too much at-home with prejudice in their churches: "Race prejudice is not the monopoly of the infidel, of the atheist, of the man of the world. It is shared equally by so-called professing Christians." For Grimké, such a state of affairs demanded one of two responses: either the white church should "disavow any connection whatever with Christianity, to repudiate it, to give it up entirely, to break absolutely with it, to say frankly: I believe in race prejudice, in these discriminations," or it ought to "bring its actual life in harmony with the great principles which it professes to accept, to believe in." Grimké asserted that genuine Christianity, backed as it is by the omnipotent power of God, is not impotent in the face of racial prejudice and that the church should abide in that power by doing something about the prejudice of society. Above all, he believed in the power of God and the gospel as a source for renewal—personal, social, moral, and spiritual. "Christianity is not clay in the hands of the world-spirit to be molded by it, but is itself to be the moulder of public sentiment and everything else." And in that sense "Christianity and Race Prejudice" is not about race prejudice per se but about the responsibility of Christian ministers, of all Christians, and of the church to resist whatever evils exist contrary to Christ with the Word of Christ and the example of Christlikeness.

The last two selections included in this volume, "The Religious Aspect of Reconstruction" (1919) and "Christ's Program for the Saving of the World" (1936), are discourses aimed directly at ministers and those preparing for ministry. These addresses offer the clearest examples of Grimké's relentless emphasis on the primacy of preaching the gospel and of living the gospel in any effort to engage the world. Speaking to colleagues in the ministry, he dwelled less on any particular social problem and offered a straightforward summation of what he understood the charge to the church to be with regard to the world's problems and the method for meeting that charge. Against the tide of proponents of the

Social Gospel, he argued, "The great function of the Christian Church is to minister to the spiritual needs of men. It may have other functions; but this is its supreme function. Its paramount obligation lies here. It is the one force or institution in the world, set up by God himself with a definite spiritual mission, to wit, to bring men back to God. . . ." To fulfill this mission, Grimké pointed his colleagues back to the one method the Lord Jesus Christ Himself bequeathed to His Church—preaching the gospel. He concluded, "The more we get away from the gospel in our preaching, and away from the teaching of the Scriptures in regard to character and conduct, the greater will be the swing away from the things that are true, just, pure, lovely and of good report." To put a finer point on the argument, Grimké admonished them saying, "If we are not going to preach the gospel, and teach the Word of God faithfully we have no business in the ministry. And the sooner we get out of it, the better."

For those who struggle today with understanding the role and work of churches confronted with social injustice, Grimké's prescriptions for the race problems of his day are applicable. He proffered that the way to defeat race prejudice was for the white church to (1) dedicate itself to the careful teaching of God's Word in educating its members and (2) to live out that Word in the world. No other power than God's living Word incarnated in the lives of His people is necessary, and this power unleashed in millions of professing Christians could change the race problem almost overnight. Indeed, nothing has ever changed individual lives and entire societies like the peacefully conquering power of the gospel of Jesus Christ rightly taught and rightly lived. And nothing has ever formed so solid a foundation upon which to build a ministry and a church.

Rev. Francis James Grimké, D.D., Pastor of 15th Street Presbyterian Church.
Photo ca. 1805..

The Afro-American Pulpit
in Relation to Race Elevation (1892)

**Delivered in 1892 before the Ministers' Union
in Washington, D.C.**

What we need most of all is character. I do not undervalue the importance of wealth—there are many things dependent upon it—many things that we cannot have without it, and therefore it is right and proper that we should think of it and seek by all honorable means to possess it. I do not undervalue education. One of the crowning glories of our humanity is that man is a thinking being, that he has a mind endowed with various faculties and capabilities, that he is capable of knowing things material and spiritual, things natural and supernatural. One of the strongest evidences of his superiority to the brute creation is to be found in the civilization with which he has surrounded himself and in the vast strides that he has made in almost every department of knowledge through this marvelous thing we call intellect. The intellect therefore should be cultivated. Schools, colleges, universities ought to be encouraged, and everything done that can be done to lead our people to avail themselves of all possible opportunities in this direction. But if we are to stand, if our rise is to be permanent, if we are not to pass away like the morning mist or wither like the grass, beneath the material and intellectual there must be a moral basis.

The house built upon the rock is the house that will stand when the rains descend and the floods come and winds blow and beat upon it. That rock is character—Christian character. That is more important to the Negro today than anything else. To make our people strong in morals is to render them invincible in the battle of life. In the Sermon on the Mount the promise is, "Seek ye first the kingdom of God, and his righteousness; and all these things shall be added unto you." What things? Jesus had just been saying to them, "Take no thought for your life . . . saying, What shall we eat? or, What shall we drink? or Wherewithal shall we be clothed? . . . your heavenly Father knoweth that ye have need of all these things." The thought is, character is the supreme thing. Put that first, make righteousness the basis of life, enter into the kingdom of God, conform to its rules and regulations, and the lesser problems will take care of themselves.

The future of the Negro, his ability to hold his own as a permanent factor in the world's civilization and against the aggressions of his enemies in this country, depends more upon character than upon anything else, and therefore it is upon that the chief emphasis should be laid. Every Negro in every part of the country by some means should be made to feel, and to feel at once, the transcendent importance of character. But how is this to be done? How are these eight million of our people to be reached, scattered as they are in every state and territory of the Union? It is a stupendous work. If one hundred men and women thoroughly consecrated to the work should begin today, each working twelve hours a day and speaking to some soul every ten minutes, it would take more than four years to cover the field. But what would a ten-minute talk once in four years amount to as a factor in the development of character? It would amount to simply nothing; and therefore if we are ever to be aroused to a proper appreciation of this subject, it must be through some agency or instrumentality that has the ear of the people and that is closely and intimately associated with them. That agency or instrumentality I believe to be the Christian ministry.

The minister is a teacher. This is the idea of the Old Testament prophet. This is the idea of the New Testament ministry. The direction given to the apostles was to lay hands suddenly on no man, to ordain to the ministry only such as were apt to teach. This was largely the mission of Christ. Much of His time was given to instruction. In the Sermon on the Mount the record is, "He opened his mouth, and taught them" [Matt. 5:2]. Again and again this is the representation made of Him.

The minister is a moral teacher. His duty is to rebuke wrong and to keep steadily before his hearers the right. His work, mainly, is character-building, to give the right direction to the budding and expanding life around him—in a word, to develop and strengthen Christian character. In sending His disciples forth, Jesus directed them to go and disciple all nations—to teach them to observe all things that He had commanded them. And the same thought is expressed in Ephesians 4:11-13, in which the aim and scope of the ministry is clearly and distinctly set forth: "He gave some, apostles; and some, prophets; and some, evangelists; and some, pastors and teachers; for the perfecting of the saints, for the work of the ministry, for the edifying of the body of Christ; till we all come in the unity of the faith, and of the knowledge of the Son of God, unto a perfect man, unto the measure of the stature of the fullness of Christ." He gave them that they might set into operation the forces that were to lift the individual and the race to the lofty plane of Christian manhood and womanhood. Hence a reference to the record will show that it was toward this end that the prophets and apostles labored almost exclusively. Read the Old Testament prophets, as well as the historical books in which the prophets mainly figure, such as 1 and 2 Samuel, 1 and 2 Kings, etc., and you will see that the emphasis throughout is laid upon character, upon right living. It is a call, from beginning to end, to turn from sin to righteousness.

Everything is done to convince men of sin, to lead them to repentance, to show them a better way. Isaiah opens his prophecy with the cry, "Wash you, make you clean; put away the evil of your doings from before mine eyes; cease to do evil; learn to do well" (Isa. 1:16-17), and that cry never ceases from beginning to end. It runs all through the prophetical books. The very last chapter of Malachi is a solemn call to righteousness:

> *For, behold, the day cometh, that shall burn as an oven; and all the proud, yea, and all that do wickedly, shall be stubble: and the day that cometh shall burn them up, saith the LORD of hosts, that it shall leave them neither root nor branch. But unto you that fear my name shall the Sun of righteousness arise with healing in his wings; and ye shall go forth, and grow up as calves of the stall. And ye shall tread down the wicked; for they shall be ashes under the soles of your feet in the day that I shall do this, saith the LORD of hosts. Remember ye the law of Moses my servant, which I commanded unto him in Horeb for all Israel, with the statutes and judgments. Behold, I will send you Elijah the prophet before the coming of the great and dreadful day of the LORD: And he shall turn the heart of the fathers to the children, and the heart of the children to their fathers, lest I come and smite the earth with a curse.*

— 4 : 1 - 6

So when we come to the New Testament, even the most casual perusal of the epistles reveals the same things. While their authors do not lose sight of the great facts in the life of Christ—His incarnation, His death upon the cross, His resurrection, the great doctrine of justification by faith, the glorious plan of salvation as wrought by Him, so that God can be just and yet the justifier of the ungodly—the offer of salvation to all freely, without money and without price, on condition of repentance and faith—utmost pains are always taken to set forth the transcendent importance of character. They never lose sight of this. They never allow an opportunity to pass without speaking of it. They bring it up again and again, in every conceivable way and on every possible occasion. Their earnestness in the matter is seen in the care that they take to go into every particular. They speak not only of sin in general but of particular sins. In such epistles as those to the Ephesians and the Corinthians sin after sin is singled out—lying, dishonesty, licentiousness, drunkenness, envy, jealousy, and the like.

And on the other hand, the virtues are also clearly presented in their teachings. They keep before the minds of their hearers the things that make for righteousness—the virtues and the graces that adorn and beautify and ennoble life. "Whatsoever things are true, whatsoever things are honest, whatsoever things are just, whatsoever things are pure, whatsoever things are lovely, whatsoever things are of good report, if there be any virtue and if there be any praise, think on these things" (Phil. 4:8) is what they said to the people as they met them day after day and week after week and month after month. It was line upon line, precept upon precept, here a little and there a little, all looking toward the one great end, the development of Christian character. Even in writing to Timothy and Titus, men who held high positions in the church and in whom the apostle had every confidence, see how careful he was to put in the forefront this idea of character:

> *This is a true saying, if a man desires the office of a bishop, he desireth a good work. A bishop then must be blameless, the husband of one wife, vigilant, sober, of good behaviour, given to hospitality, apt to teach; not given to wine, no striker, not greedy of filthy lucre; but patient, not a brawler, not covetous; one that ruleth well his own house, having his children in subjection with all gravity; (For if a man know not how to rule his own house, how shall he take care of the church of God?) Not a novice, lest being lifted up with pride he fall into the condemnation of the devil. Moreover he must have a good report of them which are without; lest he fall into reproach and the snare of the devil.*

Likewise must the deacons be grave, not double-tongued, not given to much wine, not greedy of filthy lucre; holding the mystery of the faith in a pure conscience. And let these also first be proved; then let them use the office of a deacon, being found blameless. Even so must their wives be grave, not slanderers, sober, faithful in all things. Let the deacons be the husbands of one wife, ruling their children and their own houses well.

—1 TIM. 3:1-12

Character first, last, always was the keynote struck by every apostle, prophet, and teacher mentioned in the inspired volume. It was the keynote struck by the Master Himself in the very beginning of His ministry. He opened His Sermon on the Mount with the words, "Blessed are the poor in spirit. . . . Blessed are the meek. . . . Blessed are the merciful. . . . Blessed are the pure in heart." And that is the keynote that must be struck, and struck more frequently than any other, by every minister if he is to fulfill his high mission as God's representative and is to make himself felt as a moral force in properly directing the budding and expanding life around him.

With this conception of the minister's vocation and these possibilities of ministerial usefulness before us, I desire now for a moment to take up the question as to whether this ideal is realized by the Afro-American pulpit today. Is this the kind of preaching that is done in our pulpits? Is the emphasis put where it ought to be put? Are the men occupying these pulpits themselves impressed with the transcendent importance of character, and does that appear in their pulpit ministrations, private life, and social relations? The subject is a most important one and is well worthy of the most serious consideration of all who are interested in the question of race elevation in this country. It is a question that cannot be overlooked or passed by in a discussion like this, in which we are considering the elements that stand today as impediments in the way of our progress. It appears that we have about fifteen thousand men in the ministry in the various denominations. Some of these men are well-educated, being graduates of some of our higher educational institutions, and others, though not blessed with a knowledge of the classics and higher mathematics, are well-trained in English, are men of intelligence, and are able to understand and properly expound the Word of God. Some of them are highly gifted as speakers and thinkers. Some of the finest orators to be found in our country today are on our list of Afro-American ministers. They know how to speak, how to touch the heart and move the will. The Massillons and Bourdaloues and Whitefields are not all dead yet. Nor are they confined to the ranks of their descendants.

Some of them are pure in character, men of integrity and honor who enjoy the confidence and respect of all who know them. Some of them are men of real piety, men who fear God and hate iniquity and whose aim and desire is to glorify Him.

Many of them are public-spirited men, men who love the race, who see what is needed, who see where we are weak and are laboring unselfishly and earnestly to remedy these defects. Some of them are men of great executive ability and of remarkable energy and push, men of affairs who know how to put into motion the forces that are necessary to produce great results. With such a ministry all things would be possible to us in this country; with such a ministry the outlook would indeed be promising. But unfortunately this is only one side of the picture. There is another side, which, painful as it may be, it is our duty also to present. Our ministers are not all of this stamp.

Many of them are ignorant men, men who can scarcely do more than read and write. Some of them can hardly do that. Many of them are ungodly men, men who are in the pulpit purely from selfish considerations, for what they can get out of it, and they are ready at all times to fall in with anything that will advance their personal and selfish interests, regardless of how it may affect the welfare of the people. Many of them are bad men, men with no character, men who have no moral standing. The statement made by Professor Washington some time ago as to the intellectual and moral unfitness of a large proportion of our ministers created a great sensation and brought down upon his head an avalanche of criticism and abuse; but the simple fact is, his statement has never been refuted. The testimony of the men who have had the best opportunities of knowing, who have traveled most extensively, and who are in a position to speak with authority goes to confirm, in a measure at least, the truth of the statement. They all, without exception, admit that while the picture may be a little overdrawn, while the figures may be a little too high, very much of what he says is true.

No attempt has been made, even on the part of those who assailed the professor most furiously, to wholly deny the charge of moral unfitness. In the great African Methodist General Conference, which met in Philadelphia, one of the oldest and most experienced bishops did not hesitate in a prayer of remarkable power, on the eve of the election of bishops, to say in that great assembly, in the hearing of the whole world, "God, you know there are bad men here, unprincipled men. God, defeat them!" And there *were* bad men there, and there are bad men everywhere in the church. If anyone has any doubt on this matter and will take the pains to look into it, he will not have to go very far in order to be convinced. I have seen enough myself, to say nothing of what I have gathered from a large number of competent witnesses, to convince me that the professor is not very far out of the way, that the number of bad men who have crept into our ministry is disgracefully and alarmingly large. So much for the personnel of our ministry.

If we turn now and examine carefully the character of the ministrations of the Afro-American pulpit, its three leading characteristics will be found to be emotionalism, levity or frivolity, and a greed for money. First, it is emotion. The aim seems to be to get up an excitement, to arouse the feelings, to create an audible outburst or emotion, or, in the popular phraseology, to get up a shout to make people "happy." In many churches where this result is not realized, where the minister is unable by sheer force of lung power and strength of imagination to produce this state of commotion, he is looked upon as a failure. Even where there is an attempt to instruct, in the great majority of cases this idea is almost sure to assert itself and become the dominant one.

Now, where emotionalism prevails, three things will be found to be true. First, there will be little or no instruction from the pulpit. The minister whose sole or chief aim is to get up a shout, to excite animal spirits, will not give much time to the study of God's Word or to the instruction of the people in the practical duties of religion, for two reasons: First, study is not necessary to that kind of preaching. All that is necessary is lung power, fluency of speech, and the ability to strike attitudes and make gestures. Second, the goal of such preaching would be defeated by such a course. Most of the shouting is done when the pulpit is dealing in glittering generalities or in meaningless utterances or is conjuring up pictures that appeal purely to the imagination. It is when the minister is speaking of golden streets and pearly gates and white robes and a land flowing with milk and honey that the noise is greatest.

Everything is quiet enough when the theme is practical Christianity, when some Elijah stands forth and in the name of God puts the line to the plumb and says, "This is wrong, and that is wrong; turn from the evil of your ways." When the theme is honesty in business, truthfulness, purity, temperance, the duty of husbands and wives to their families and to each other, the duty of parents to properly train their children—when the theme is brotherhood and sympathy and righteousness, the duty of honoring God by upright, consistent, godly lives, there is not much danger of being disturbed by a great amount of noise. People do not shout and get happy over the Ten Commandments or the Sermon on the Mount or the thirteenth chapter of First Corinthians. That kind of preaching and emotionalism do not go together. It is only when the minister gets away from the earth and from the practical, everyday duties of life, from applied Christianity, into the air, somewhere near the pearly gates, that noise begins. That in itself shows the utter hollowness of the whole thing. If emotionalism came to the surface when there was work to be done, when there were responsibilities to be assumed and sacrifices to be made, a ministry that encouraged it would be indeed a blessing; but under the present circumstances, it is an evil and is to be greatly deplored.

Second, where emotionalism prevails, there will be a low state of spirituality among the people, and necessarily so. Christian character is not built up in that way. Such growth comes from the knowledge and practice of Christian principles. If the body is to grow, it must be fed, and fed on wholesome and nutritious food. The same is true of the soul; and that food is God's Word, line upon line and precept upon precept. There is no other way of getting out of the bogs and malarious atmosphere of selfishness and pride and ill will and hatred and the many things that degrade and brutalize into the higher regions of love and purity and obedience and felicity except by the assimilation of Christian principles, except by holy and loving obedience to the will of God. We cannot get up there on the wings of emotion; we cannot shout ourselves up to a high Christian manhood and womanhood any more than we can shout ourselves into heaven. We must grow up to it. And until this fact is distinctly understood and fully appreciated and allowed to have its weight in our pulpit ministrations, the plane of spirituality upon which the masses of our people move will continue to be low. Shouting is not religion. The ability to make a noise is no test of Christian character. The noisiest Christians are not the most saintly; those who shout the most vigorously are not always the most exemplary in character and conduct.

Third, where emotionalism prevails, the underlying conception of religion will be found to be false, pernicious, and degrading. The conception that James gives us of religion is this: "Pure religion and undefiled before God and the Father is this, To visit the fatherless and widows in their affliction, and to keep himself unspotted from the world" [1:27]. The conception that Paul gives is, "Covet earnestly the best gifts: and yet shew I unto you a more excellent way" [1 Cor. 12:31]. Also, "Charity suffereth long, and is kind" [1 Cor. 13:4], etc. The conception that Micah gives is, "What doth the LORD require of thee, but to do justly, and to love mercy, and to walk humbly with thy God?" (Micah 6:8). The conception that the blessed Lord Himself gives is, "For I was an hungered, and ye gave me meat: I was thirsty, and ye gave me drink. . . . I was sick, and in prison . . . and ye came unto me" (Matt. 25:35-36). Running through all these statements of principles, the dominant, controlling idea, is character. In emotionalism, however, this element is entirely overlooked or sinks almost entirely out of sight. The measure of one's piety is made to depend upon the strength and the amount of his emotions. Thus the true ideal is shut out from view, the standard set up is a false one, and the result is not only stagnation but degradation. The ideal of religion that is held up in our pulpits, and that is cherished by the people, must be in harmony with the facts as revealed in the Word of God if it is to have an elevating and ennobling effect upon their everyday life.

The second characteristic of the Afro-American pulpit is levity, frivolity, a lack of seriousness. There is entirely too much place given to making fun, to joking, to exciting laughter. The minister too often becomes a jester, a buffoon, a clown. Thus all solemnity is destroyed, and the House of God in many cases becomes a mere playhouse for the entertainment or amusement of the people. This has become so prevalent in many of our churches that the people have come to expect it with the same regularity as they expect to hear preaching. If the minister after he has preached before closing does not make a fool of himself and set the people grinning, a sense of disappointment and incompleteness is felt. Again and again I have sat in churches and have been saddened and disgusted by what I have seen in this direction. And the most serious part of it all is that this levity comes at the very time when it is most baneful. If it came before preaching, it would not be quite so bad, though even then it would be a thing to be regretted. But coming as it does after the sermon, the effect is to entirely obliterate whatever good impression has been made and thus to defeat the very purpose for which the church has been organized. Sometimes I have said, what is the use of preaching—why not introduce the buffoon, the clown, at once, and when he is through bring the service to a close?

The third characteristic of the Afro-American pulpit is a greed for money. Everything seems to be arranged with reference to the collection. The great objective point seems to be to reach the pocketbooks of the people. Here is where the greatest amount of interest is manifested; here is where there is the greatest concentration of energy. However tame the services may be up to this point, here everybody seems to wake up, and new life seems to be infused into everything, as if to say, "Now is the time when the real business for which we have met will begin." There is no harm, of course, in raising money. The church cannot get along without it. Its just debts must be paid; its obligations must be met. The complaint is not against raising money but against the abuse of this, against the undue prominence that is given to it in the Afro-American pulpit. It overshadows every other interest. The ability to raise money is more highly esteemed than the ability to preach the Word effectively. The greatest financier, the most successful money-gatherer, receives the best place and is most highly esteemed by those in authority. The result is, the church is rapidly becoming a mere institution for raising money, with preaching, singing, and praying being only incidental, and the ministry is rapidly degenerating into a mere agency for begging. The perceived problem is not how to elevate the people, how to bring them into the Kingdom of Christ, how to save them from their sins and sanctify them, but how to get their money.

A ministry whose chief characteristics are emotionalism, frivolity, and greed for money is not a ministry to inspire hope and is not a source of strength but of weakness. And this is the charge I make against the Afro-American pulpit today. It is not living up to its opportunities; it is not doing the work that it ought to do. It is not putting the emphasis where it ought to be put. It is frittering away its energies upon things of minor importance, to the neglect of those things that are fundamental and without which we cannot hope for any permanent prosperity. And this is why as a people we have made so little progress morally. The fault is due very largely to the character of our pulpit ministrations. If there had been less effort made at emotional effects and less jesting and less prominence given to finances and more time and attention given to the great fundamental principles of religion and morality (the bedrock upon which character is built) and to the patient, painstaking instruction of the people in the practical duties of life, the outlook would be very much brighter than it is today. The moral plane upon which the masses of our people move is confessedly not very high and in view of their past antecedents could not be expected to be high. But if they had had the proper kind of instruction from the pulpit, there is every reason to believe that they would stand very much higher today than they do. The thing most to be deplored in our condition today is not our poverty, nor our ignorance, but our moral deficiencies, and for these deficiencies the Afro-American pulpit is in a very large measure responsible. The very fact that our people have had a long schooling in slavery, the tendency of which has been to blunt the moral sensibilities and to degrade the whole moral nature, makes it all the more important that special attention should be given to their development in this direction and renders the character of much of our pulpit ministration all the more reprehensible.

In palliation of this it has been said, I know, that the people prefer the noise and excitement that come from ranting and bluster. There may be some truth in this, but the mission of the pulpit is not to cater to the vitiated tastes of the people and is not to give them what they want but what they ought to have—to lift up a standard for them, to set before them right and wrong, whether it accords with their tastes or not. The plea that the people prefer a certain thing can never be an excuse or justification for giving them that thing unless it is good in itself, unless it would be beneficial to them. The problem that the Afro-American pulpit has to solve is not what will be most congenial to the people but what will be most helpful to them; not what kind of preaching they like best but what kind of preaching will be the most effective in developing in them a true manhood and womanhood, in making them good fathers and mothers, good husbands and wives, good citizens and neighbors, what kind of preaching will yield the largest returns in purity, honesty, sobriety, sweetness, gentleness. And the pulpit that has the wisdom to answer this question intelligently and the courage to act out its convictions is the pulpit that we need and that we must have if "on stepping-stones of our dead selves" we are "to rise to higher things" [Booker T. Washington].

Christianity and Race Prejudice
(June 5, 1910)

How is it that thou, being a Jew, askest drink of me, which am a woman of Samaria? for the Jews have no dealings with Samaritans.

— JOHN 4:9

In the sermon on the last Sabbath I spoke of what race prejudice is, of what Christianity is, and of the attitude of Christianity toward race prejudice, as indicated in the character of Jesus Christ and in the great principles of the Christian religion, such as the Fatherhood of God, the brotherhood of man, the Golden Rule, loving one's neighbor as one's self, following things that make for peace and edification, and the unity of all believers in Christ. The discussion brought out the fact that every principle of Christianity, every sentiment of true religion, is totally, absolutely opposed to race prejudice in every shape and form.

Such being the case, I pass on in the next place to ask: What is the attitude of the church toward race prejudice? By the church I mean the religious denominations that stand as the visible and organized representatives of Christianity, of the great principles of which I have been speaking. I mean the men and women who make up the membership of our churches—the men and women who profess to be Christians. There are in this country thirty million such professing Christians; and in connection with these churches, under their care and supervision, are some fifteen million Sunday school scholars who are being instructed in the knowledge of the Word of God, who are being trained for membership in the Kingdom of Jesus Christ. The question I am asking is, what is the attitude of this great body of Christians who have pledged themselves to embody, in their own personal character and lives, and to endeavor to get others to do the same, the great principles of the Christian religion, who have pledged themselves to follow Jesus Christ, through evil report and through good report? What is their attitude in regard to this evil, this ever-growing evil, in this great Republic of ours?

The information that I am seeking here is not what public declarations have been made, occasionally, in the form of resolutions or otherwise by denominations or public gatherings touching this matter, but what is the practice of the congregations that make up these denominations and of the men who occupy their pulpits? Do they welcome people of all races to their places of worship, to their Sabbath schools, to the Endeavor Societies, and to membership in their churches? Do they treat people of all races, when they come into their assemblies, with the same courtesy, the same cordiality? What is the practice, as individuals, of the millions of professing Christians in their contact with men of other races? Are they influenced in the treatment that they accord to them in the street, on streetcars, in places of public resort, in all the relations of life, by this feeling of race prejudice or by the principles of the religion that they profess to accept and to believe in? Are these millions of professing Christians in their homes, in their places of business, in public and in private, throwing the weight of their individual personal influence for or against this evil of race prejudice? Are they exemplifying in their individual personal character and lives, in dealing with this question, the spirit of the Master whom they profess to be serving or the spirit of the world, of the evil one, of the prince of the powers of darkness? In other words, is the attitude of the average white church in this country, and the average white professor of religion, on this subject consistent with the religion that they profess?

In seeking an answer to these questions, it is the truth that we want to know, and nothing but the truth, whether it makes for us or against us, whether we like it or not, for it is the truth alone that will make us free. What we want to know is, what are the facts in the case?

So far as the practice of churches or congregations is concerned, race prejudice is in almost absolute control. In the whole southern section of our country it absolutely dominates the situation. In all that southern land there is scarcely a white church, be it said to the shame of those churches, where a colored person would be accorded anything like decent treatment; there is scarcely one in which a colored person would be received as a beloved brother, however exemplary might be his conduct, however saintly might be his character. In most of them he would not be received at all; in a few he might be received, provided he was willing to be thrust away into the gallery or some obscure corner, set apart particularly for his kind. The reception of colored children into

Sabbath schools and Endeavor Societies in these churches would not, of course, be considered for a moment.

As to other sections of our country, things are not quite so bad, but they are bad enough and are getting steadily worse. The white churches of the North, as a general thing, are no more kindly disposed toward the attendance of colored people at their services than the churches in the South. They may not decline to seat a colored person if he goes, but they will treat him in such a way as to make him know very distinctly that he is not welcomed, that his absence would be preferable to his presence. That is not true of all, but it is true of a very large number, and a growing number. Even in a church like Trinity, Boston—the church over which the sainted Phillips Brooks once presided, and where during his pastorate men of all races were equally welcomed—the black brother no longer feels at home there, is no longer made welcome there. The simple fact is, colored people are not wanted in white churches, in white Sabbath schools, in white Endeavor Societies, in white religious societies of any kind. The simple fact is, when they venture occasionally into these churches, they are not treated with the same courtesy, with the same cordiality, as white people are treated.

The feeling is, "Why don't you colored people attend your own churches?" Jesus said, "My house shall be called the house of prayer for all nations" [Mark 11:17], but that is not true of the average white church in this country. It is not a house of prayer for all nations, but only for white men and white women and white children, only for members of the white race. That is the feeling that pervades them, that dominates them. "For white people only" is what is inscribed over the portals of most of them, as interpreted by the prevailing sentiment within them. This may be denied, but no denial can alter the fact. An honest expression of sentiment on the part of the members of these churches, however deplorable it might be, however unfavorable may be the light in which it may place them as professing Christians, will be found to be in accord with what I have said. Most of these churches have built into them the idea that they are for white people and not for colored people. Most of these churches are pervaded by the sentiment that does not look kindly upon the idea of the introduction of colored people into their religious organizations and gatherings; underlying most of them is the caste of feeling, growing out of race prejudice.

If anyone has any doubt on the matter, all that is necessary to be done in order to get at the truth is to let some colored person apply for membership in most of them and see what the result would be. I venture the assertion that, with here and there perhaps an exception, such an application would not be received with favor, with any degree of cordiality, as would be the case had it come from a white person. The application, if it were not out-and-out denied, would be deferred, and efforts would be made to dissuade the applicant from pressing it, to induce him to change his mind and seek admission elsewhere. I have in mind now such an application that was made to one of the prominent churches in this city. Everything was in due form, but the application was "not received." The party did not succeed in getting in. One excuse and another was found, among them that she would feel more at home among her own people. In other words, she was given to understand, if not in so many words, but just as clearly, that the church was for white people and not for colored people.

The spirit that this incident brings out in connection with that particular church is true of most of the white churches. It is clearly understood by their officers, by their members, and by the men who fill their pulpits that they are for white people and not for colored people. And the reason why we have white churches and colored churches, white Sunday schools and colored Sunday schools, white Endeavor Societies and colored Endeavor Societies, is because of race prejudice. This line of cleavage has been drawn, this difference has been made, out of deference to race prejudice; this aspect of the churches' policy has been dictated by race antipathy. Everywhere this hydra-headed monster has not only intruded itself but is in control.

Why should there be churches made up of white Christians and churches made up of colored Christians in the same community, where all speak the same language? Why should white Christians and colored Christians not feel perfectly at home with each other in the same religious gatherings, if they are all Christians, if they all believe in the Fatherhood of God and the brotherhood of man, in doing by others as they would be done by, in loving each other as they love themselves, in their oneness in Christ Jesus, and if the same Holy Spirit dwells alike in all their hearts? With these great principles guiding, directing, and influencing them, that would be what you would naturally expect to find, just as in all churches you find all classes and conditions brought together—rich and poor, high and low, educated and uneducated. Any attempt to build the Christian church on any of these lines exclusively would be recognized at once as wrong, as contrary to the spirit of Jesus Christ. You can't say this church is for rich people only or for educated people only or for people of position or high social station only and call it Christian. A church run in any such spirit would be obviously against every principle of Christianity. And yet all over this country are churches, calling themselves Christian in spirit and practice, for white people only, churches where colored people are not desired.

The fact that such is the case and is a fact calls for an explanation. What is the explanation of this unnatural condition of things that we find all over our land in so-called Christian churches? Why are all on the inside of some of them white and all on the inside of others black? Why this indisposition of one group of persons to mingle with another group in churches, in religious gatherings, in the worship of God? The great reason—there may be others—is to be found in race prejudice. The underlying fact out of which this situation grows is the difference of race; and this difference has been one of the great determining factors in the organized church life of the nation, one of its most conspicuous characteristics. The lines have been set up not where Jesus Christ directs them to be set up but where race prejudice dictates that they should be set up. The principles of the world have controlled, have been allowed to determine, what shall be and shall not be, instead of the principles of the great Head of the church.

As to the practice of the individuals who make up this great body of professing Christians, in their contact, in their relation with men of other races, the same is true: race prejudice is in almost absolute control; its influence almost everywhere dominates.

People who are content to be identified with churches such as I have been describing—churches that don't want colored people in them, that would rather have them stay away from their services—are not likely to treat them with any more consideration when they meet them elsewhere. If Afro-Americans are not good enough to worship with them in the same sanctuary, they are not likely to think any better of them when they meet them on the outside. People who want separate churches are likely also to want separate schools and separate hotels and separate restaurants and separate cars and separate everything. If churches, which are supposed to be the center of the religious life of the community and therefore to represent the highest standard of what is right in their very structure in the lines upon which they are organized, teach that men are to be shunned, are to be excluded, are to be discriminated against because of race or color, the individual members are not likely to have any higher standard, are not likely to act on any higher principle. People who in their church life get the idea of race superiority, of race exclusiveness, will be likely to carry it with them in the wider relations outside the church.

This, as a matter of fact, is what we find to be actually true. Race prejudice is not the monopoly of the infidel, the atheist, or the man of the world. It is shared equally by so-called professing Christians. The men who have been most active in promoting Jim Crow streetcar legislation, in bringing about all forms of discrimination, in holding the Afro-American race up to contempt, in saying the bitterest things against it, have not all been outside the church. Many of them have not only been in the church but have held high places in it. The simple fact is, there is no appreciable difference, in the great majority of cases, in the exhibition of race prejudice, in the treatment that is accorded to people of color, between those who profess to be Christians and those who make no profession. The fact that they are members of Christian churches, that they are professing Christians, exerts no appreciable influence over them. It is a thing entirely apart from their religion, a thing that does not involve in the least any religious principle. They do not seem to see any inconsistency between the two things. All the high and holy principles of the Christian religion, they seem to think, have reference only to or are in force only when they have dealings with members of their own race. It is surprising how little influence the religion of Jesus Christ has had in controlling the prejudice of men, in lifting them above the low plane upon which race prejudice places them.

On the block where I am living, which is one of the longest blocks in the city, a few years ago every house on it, on both sides, was occupied by white people. Today there is only one white family to be found in it. There has been an almost complete exodus. Just as soon as one colored family got in, the excitement began; and when a second got in, it almost created a panic. One by one these white people

Folded their tents like the Arabs,
And silently stole away.

Many of them were members of Christian churches; one of them was a relative of a retired minister of the gospel. These church members, these professing Christians, were unwilling to even live in the same block with colored people, though they had no personal contact with them and though among those colored neighbors were three colored ministers, pastors of three of the leading colored churches of this city. This indisposition to live even on the same block with colored people is just as prevalent among professing Christians as among the non-professing. And it doesn't make any difference as to the grade of colored persons, as to how intelligent, how refined, how well-to-do, how unobjectionable in point of character they may be—the indisposition is just as strong.

These are all the facts, indisputable facts. And these facts of experience and observation—facts that lie all around us, within easy reach of anybody—prove conclusively that the Christian church in this land, in its organized capacity and in the life of the individuals that make up its membership, is very largely under the power of this degrading and un-Christian sentiment of race prejudice. It is a humiliating confession to make, but it is true—the church today is the great bulwark of race prejudice in this country. It is doing more than any other single agency to uphold it, to make it respectable, to encourage people to continue in it. It not only upholds it within its own peculiar institutions but furnishes an example to the non-believing world to do the same. So both within and without [outside], its influence, its example, tells mightily in favor of these discriminations, these invidious distinctions, based upon race, upon color.

In the light of these facts, in view of the actual condition of things as we find it in this land, I raise the question, and it is a question that the church itself ought to consider, is it occupying the position that it ought to occupy in this matter? Is it standing where it ought to stand? Is it standing where Jesus Christ would have it stand? In other words, is its present attitude on the race question right or wrong? To this question, in the light of what Christianity is, in the light of who Jesus Christ is, in spirit, in temper, in all that He said and did, there can be but one answer, a negative one. Its attitude is not what it ought to be; it is not standing where it ought to stand. It is recreant to its great trust as the light of the world; the light within it, on this point, is darkness, is misleading.

Therefore the church ought to do one of two things: (1) It ought to disavow any connection whatever with Christianity, to repudiate it, to give it up entirely, to break absolutely with it, to say frankly, "I believe in race prejudice, in these discriminations. I don't want to worship with colored people. I don't want to live on the same street with them. I don't think they are entitled to the same treatment as white people are entitled to. I am not willing to receive them as brothers religiously or otherwise. At the same time I know that Christianity teaches the Fatherhood of God and the brotherhood of man, that we should love our neighbor as ourselves, that we should do by others as we would be done by. I know that race prejudice is not in accordance with the spirit of Jesus Christ. I am not going to give up race prejudice, however; I am not going to treat these people differently than I am. If I can't hold onto race prejudice and also to Christianity at the same time, I will give up Christianity. I will not live a lie. I will not misrepresent it by continuing my connection with it." American Christianity is in honor bound to take that position, to cease to call itself Christian. Or,

(2) It ought to repent; it ought to do differently; it ought to strive to bring its actual life into harmony with the great principles that it professes to accept, to believe in. There is a need today for some John the Baptist to go all over this land, in all of the white churches, among the millions of professing Christians in them, and cry aloud, "Repent, repent. Cease to be ruled by race prejudice, to make race or color the condition of entrance into your religious activities, your organizations and gatherings. Cease this anti-Christian race feeling, and let brotherly love prevail." "Let the wicked man forsake his ways, and the unrighteous man his thoughts" (Isa. 55:7)—that is what God says, and that has reference to the man within the church as well as the man outside it. If race prejudice is wrong, then the church must forsake it, must give it up. There is no option left to it. It must repent; it must do differently; it must change its course if it is to remain Christian.

Assuming now that it is willing to do this, that it recognizes the un-Christian character of race prejudice, that it sees that it is wrong, the practical question remains to be considered: In what way may it set itself to work to overcome it? What can it do? What should it do?

(1) It ought to wake up to the fact that it can do something and that it ought to do something. Race prejudice is an evil that the church of God ought to grapple with. It ought not to sit quietly in the midst of it and do nothing. Its very silence, its lack of effort, its non-interference, to put it in its mildest form, would be construed as approving of it, or at least as not disapproving of it. The church of God can do something. There are thirty-two million professing Christians in this country, and there are over two hundred thousand men of education, many of them of the highest culture, in the pulpits of the land. These millions of professing Christians wield a tremendous influence; there isn't anything that they set their minds upon that they cannot bring about, that they cannot accomplish. The fact that it has done little or nothing toward fighting this evil has been not from lack of power but from lack of disposition. And this lack of disposition has arisen from two reasons: first, because of the presence of race prejudice in the church itself, in the hearts of those who make up the church; and second, because of cowardice, because to have done so would have run counter to an adverse public sentiment outside the church.

That the church, the membership of the church collectively and individually, has done little or nothing toward fighting this evil is evident from the damning fact that while the membership of these churches has gone on steadily increasing, side by side with that is the fact that race prejudice has gone on steadily increasing. The church has grown, and with its growth this diabolical spirit of race prejudice has also grown. The very opposite of this is what we would naturally have expected to find—with the growth of the Christian church, not an increase but a decrease of race antipathy. This strange fact, for it is a strange fact—there is nothing in the nature of Christianity that would lead us to expect any such result—ought to be an eye-opener to Christian men and women all over this country, ought to give them pause, ought to lead them to ask themselves the question, what must be the quality of the Christianity that is represented in their character and lives if such be the case? Of this strange fact there are only three possible explanations: Either Christianity is no match for race prejudice, is powerless before it; or the Christianity represented in the white churches of America is an inferior Christianity, is not genuine, is not what it purports to be; or the church has not been doing its duty, has been putting its light under a bushel, has not been faithful to its divine commission.

That real Christianity is powerless in the presence of race prejudice is not true; back of it is the mighty power of God. The gates of hell cannot prevail against it. That the Christianity represented in white America is spurious, I am not prepared to say. That the church has failed to do its duty, in this matter, I am prepared, however, to say. Had it been true to its great commission, had it lived up to its opportunities, had it stood squarely and uncompromisingly for Christian principles, the sad, the humiliating, the disgraceful fact of which we are speaking never would have been possible. The fact that in Christian America, in this land that is adding church members by the millions, race prejudice has gone on steadily increasing is a standing indictment of the white Christianity of this land—an indictment that ought to bring the blush of shame to the faces of the men and women who are responsible for it, whose silence, whose quiet acquiescence, whose cowardice, or, worse, whose active cooperation have made it possible. The first thing for the church to do, I say, is to wake up to the fact that it can do something. Its present attitude is a disgrace to it and is utterly unworthy of the name that it bears.

(2) The church ought to begin to do something. What can it do? In what way or ways may it help overthrow this giant evil? It can help to do it in the same way as Jesus sought to meet race antipathy and an adverse and unrighteous public sentiment in His day. Race hatred was just as strong in His day as it is today. The Jews had the same contempt for the Samaritan, felt the same aversion to him, as the white man feels for the Negro in this country. If possible, the feeling of antipathy was even stronger. In the midst of the society in which Jesus lived and moved there was the strongest possible feeling of aversion to certain classes known as publicans and sinners. When he said, "Zaccheus, make haste, and come down; for to day I must abide at thy house" (Luke 19:5), they threw their hands up in holy horror, saying, "He is going to be a guest of a man who is a sinner." When he permitted the woman to anoint his feet as he sat at meat in the Pharisee's house, the Pharisee expressed his astonishment in the words, "This man, if he were a prophet, would have known who and what manner of woman this is that toucheth him: for she is a sinner" (Luke 7:39). In the midst of such conditions Jesus began His great life's work. Did He fall in with the prejudices of his time? Did He allow Himself

to be controlled by the unrighteous public sentiment about Him? No. He did the very opposite of that. He showed clearly, unmistakably where He stood, what His principles were. And this He did in two ways—by what He taught and by the life He lived.

(a) By what He taught. The great principles that He declared, which He everywhere promulgated, were directly and fundamentally opposed to the evils around Him. These principles could not be accepted, could not be followed without changing conditions for the better, without bringing men closer together, without breaking down walls of separation, without infusing into all a more kindly spirit. Jesus gave a great deal of time to teaching. The rubbish of tradition—men-made opinions—had covered up the truth of God, and Jesus gave a good deal of time to clearing away this rubbish and letting the truth shine forth. In the Sermon on the Mount we have a specimen of the kind of work He did. "Ye have heard that it hath been said, Thou shalt love thy neighbour, and hate thine enemy. But I say unto you, Love your enemies, bless them that curse you, do good to them that hate you, and pray for them which despitefully use you, and persecute you" (Matt. 5:43-44). Jesus was a teacher sent from God. What He taught were the truths of God. His aim was to bring men into contact with the mind of God, with the great thoughts, feelings, and sentiments that tend to lift men Godward and heavenward instead of encouraging them in their evil inclinations and desires, in their petty prejudices and meanness. What He taught tended ever to make men broader, more liberal, more humane, more sympathetic, more kind, more loving. Jesus was a great teacher—great in the manner in which He taught and in what He taught—in the character of the truths that He declared. In what He said, in the words that fell from His lips, men knew where He stood on all the great moral issues of His day; they knew what His sentiments were, where His sympathies were.

(b) Jesus revealed His attitude and thus sought to improve conditions not only by what He taught but also, and particularly, by the life that He lived, by His personal character and conduct. In no way did He ever give countenance—by anything He did, by the manner in which He conducted Himself—to the unjust sentiments, the unholy prejudices about Him. His life, as he lived it day by day, as He came in contact with men of all classes, was always and everywhere a living protest against all the evils about Him. He never allowed Himself to be influenced by the prejudices of those around Him, by their likes and dislikes. Jesus was all the time doing unpopular things, things that public sentiment did not endorse; and He did them in order that people might know where He stood, that He was not in accord with public sentiment, that He did not approve of popular prejudices. Hence He went to dine with Zaccheus. Hence when He came to select His twelve disciples, He chose Matthew, the publican, to be one of them. Hence when He was on His way to Jerusalem, instead of going around Samaria He went through it; and when He met the Samaritan woman at Jacob's well, instead of shunning her, although the Jews had no dealings with the Samaritans, He talked to her and asked her to give Him a drink of water. And when the Samaritans, in large numbers, came out to meet Him, instead of running away from them, He received them gladly and permitted Himself to be entertained by them in their village for a day or two.

After all, the most effective way of working in the interest of reform, in seeking to change conditions for the better, is the one set forth here. It is well enough to preach, to make public declarations, to issue manifestoes bearing upon the evils to be removed; but these public declarations, these generalized statements, are soon forgotten. But where the individual life is all right, where it meets the issue squarely by consistently and persistently living out the principle that it wishes to triumph, you have a force that is ever active—silently, it may be, but ever and always working toward the goal. It is the individual life, set right in regard to this or any other matter, that counts most. And no one understood this better than the Lord Jesus Christ. Hence in His individual personal character and life He was always true to principle. His life always pointed in the direction of the principles that He advocated. He was always a living embodiment of what He taught; and hence He became a force, in the regeneration of society, that no mere words, however wise or eloquent, ever could have made Him.

In dealing with this matter of race prejudice, if the church in America—I mean our white fellow Christians—really want to get rid of it, really want to begin in earnest a crusade in the interest of true Christian brotherhood, regardless of race, color, or previous condition of servitude, the way to do it is clearly indicated in the course pursued by Jesus Christ in dealing with similar conditions in His day.

(1) There must be careful instruction. The great principles of

Christianity that are opposed to race prejudice, everything in the Word
of God that runs counter to it, that tends to set it forth in its true light as
a thing hateful to God and injurious to man, should be carefully set forth,
line upon line, precept upon precept, here a little and there a little. Some
teaching must be done; careful, painstaking instruction as to the mind of
God on this matter, as revealed in His character and in the teachings of
His Word, must be given. If race prejudice is wrong, if it is un-Christian,
unbrotherly, then that fact ought to be declared. There ought to be no
blinking on the matter, no dodging of the issue. It ought to be properly
characterized; it ought to be set forth in its true character. And this ought
to be done not with bated breath, not behind closed doors, not in secret
where no one will hear, but openly, publicly; it ought to be proclaimed
from the housetops. God directed the prophet to "cry aloud, spare not,
lift up thy voice like a trumpet" [Isa. 58:1]. And race prejudice as an evil,
hateful to God and injurious to man, ought to be proclaimed in trumpet-
tones all over the land, in every city and village and hamlet.

This work of education, of instruction, in regard to this evil should
be from the pulpit, in the Sabbath schools, in Christian Endeavor
Societies, in all Christian homes. What an opportunity is here presented
to Christian ministers, to Sunday school teachers, to leaders of Endeavor
Societies, to Christian fathers and mothers to pour in the light of divine
truth, to begin the work of regeneration, by implanting in the hearts and
minds of those who are entrusted to their care and so come under their
influence correct ideas on this matter.

The opportunity along these several lines of helping in this matter
is great. To what extent is it being utilized? How many of the more than
two hundred thousand ministers in the pulpits of this land have sought
to instruct the members of their congregations, to set them right on this
matter? How many are doing it now? In how many of these pulpits has
there been any serious attempt made to stem this tide of race prejudice
by patient, painstaking instruction out of God's Word? How many of the
thousands upon thousands of teachers in the Sunday schools connected
with these churches have done anything, directly or indirectly, to help
their scholars see the evil of race prejudice, to lead them to think more
kindly of people of color? How many of the leaders in the thousands of
Endeavor Societies in all these churches have done anything to set the
millions of young people over whom they preside right on this matter?

FRANCIS J. GRIMKÉ

Onward, Christian soldiers,
Marching as to war,
With the cross of Jesus
Going on before.

We hear them often singing these words as their battle cry. How far, to what extent is this great army of young endeavorers being trained to wage war against this ever active, ever present foe of God and man—race prejudice? How far are they being trained by the leaders to look upon race prejudice as an enemy against which the forces of religions ought to be directed? How far are Christian parents, in their homes, with their children around them, seeking to put into their hearts and minds such principles as will lift them above race prejudice, as will set them right on this matter?

There is every reason to believe that neither ministers nor Sabbath school teachers nor Endeavor leaders nor Christian parents have done very much in this direction. The children, the boys and girls, the young men and women who are coming up are just as full of prejudice as the older ones. And yet these children, these young people, are members of these churches, of these Sabbath schools, of these Endeavor Societies, of these Christian homes. If any instruction is going on in them at all with this end in view, there is no visible evidence of it. Those who are doing the teaching must be very poor teachers, or else these young people must be very inapt scholars, very dull of apprehension. The simple fact is, they are not learning to look upon race prejudice as an evil in these churches, in these Sabbath schools, in these Endeavor Societies, in these Christian homes; they are learning the very opposite. The older white Christians are dying out, but race prejudice is not dying out; it survives in their children, and it survives in their children because it lived in them, and it will continue to survive in the children as long as it lives in the parents.

I am fully persuaded that if there is ever to be a change for the better, this process of education, of careful instruction, has to begin—in the pulpit, in Sabbath schools, in Endeavor Societies, in homes. In all these centers of influence the good work has to begin, and ought to begin at once. Definite, specific instruction as to the un-Christian character of race prejudice ought to be given, and given by the Christian church, by the men and women who profess to be Christians, and given to their children and to the young people who are growing up.

148

(2) Jesus Christ not only taught the truth by word of mouth but lived it. His life and His personal character witnessed to the truth that He proclaimed. He wasn't afraid of public sentiment; He wasn't afraid to do the unpopular thing when duty required it, when loyalty to principle made it necessary. And this is the kind of testimony that our white fellow Christians must bear to the evil of race prejudice if their influence is to count for anything, if this evil is to be overcome. It isn't what they say but what they do, how they act, that will tell most. It is the testimony of the individual life, free from race prejudice, that is the important thing in this warfare that is to be waged in the interest of true brotherhood, of a larger charity. It is only as the individual Christian separates himself or herself from the accursed thing that any real progress will be made. It is the protest of the individual personal life that is needed in all these churches, Sabbath schools, Endeavor Societies, and Christian homes.

Let me now, in closing, revert for a moment to the text of Scripture with which I began this discourse. "How is it that thou being a Jew, askest drink of me who am a Samaritan woman?" (John 4:9). This woman recognized at once that there was something here quite out of the ordinary; that here was a Jew who was entirely unlike the Jews that she was in the habit of meeting. Here was a Jew who not only talked with her but asked her for a drink of water, a personal favor. The Jews had no dealings with the Samaritans; the Jews despised the Samaritans. She finds nothing like this, however, in this man; she finds in him an entirely different spirit. It puzzles her; she doesn't know what to make of it. So she says frankly to him, "How is it—explain yourself—that you, a Jew, treat me in the manner in which you do, so unlike your fellow countrymen?" The question is an interesting one and has in it an important lesson for our white American Christians. What was it that made the difference between Jesus and the ordinary Jew? The answer comes out in what follows. In answer to her question Jesus began to reveal Himself to her. How so?

(a) In His wonderful knowledge, in the insight that He had into her past life and history. "Come, see a man, which told me all things that ever I did" is what she said (John 4:29). She saw that He was no ordinary individual.

(b) Impressed with his wonderful insight, she said, "I perceive thou art a prophet," a man of God; and then naturally she glided on to the great thought of the Messiah, the hope of all the ages, the long-promised Deliverer. And then it was that Jesus said to her, "I that speak unto thee am he." She was talking with the Messiah, though she knew it not.

(c) And then as the conversation went on He spoke of a wonderful water that He wanted to give her—the water of life, which, if a man drinks it, he will never thirst again, for it would be in him a well of water springing up into everlasting life. And then He went on to declare to her the great truth that "The hour cometh, and now is, when the true worshippers shall worship the Father in spirit and in truth: for the Father seeketh such to worship him. God is a spirit: and they that worship him must worship him in spirit and in truth" (John 4:23-24). Not at Jerusalem, nor in Samaria would it be necessary for men to meet in order to render acceptable worship to God, but everywhere, among all races and nations, the sincere worshiper was acceptable unto him. The conception that He gives us here of God and of what constitutes acceptable worship transcends the thought of race or nationality and lifts us at once out of the narrow racial groove in which both Jew and Samaritan were in the habit of moving into the higher conception of fitness, of character, in which all men must stand in order to be acceptable to God. It was not whether a man was a Jew or a Gentile about which God cared and that counted with him, but the character of the worship that he rendered, the state of his heart. This was the way God felt, and this was the way Jesus felt as His representative on earth. The reason why His treatment of the Samaritan woman was different from the treatment that an ordinary Jew would have accorded her is manifest for these reasons:

(1) It was because He was the Messiah and stood as such in relation to all the races of mankind. He was the Light of the World—the light to lighten the Gentiles and the glory of Israel—and therefore Jew and Gentile alike appealed to him. (2) It was because He was what He was in point of character, because His principles were what they were, because of the great purpose that dominated His life.

He came to redeem the world, to bring men back to God—to a recognition of Him and of the great standard of character and conduct that He had set up for the government of all. He came to break down walls of separation and to make all men brethren. Being what He was, His principles being what they were, His treatment of the Samaritan woman was perfectly natural, just what was should have been expected.

The latter part of the text is, "The Jews have no dealings with the Samaritans." And this represents substantially the condition that exists between whites and blacks in this country. So far as their religious and social relations are concerned, the white people have no dealings with the colored people. This is true of the whites within the church as well as those outside it. Just as the Jews felt toward the Samaritans, the whites feel toward the colored people in this country. If, however, the church was all right, if these whites professing religion were all right, if they were true to the principles of the Christian religion, in their treatment of the colored people they would stand apart from the other white people in this country, just as Jesus stood apart from the rest of the Jews around Him in his treatment of this Samaritan woman. But they do not stand apart. They are indistinguishable from them; they are in no respect different from them. To how many of the white Christians in this country could it be truthfully said by any number of colored people, "How is it that you, being white, treat us as brethren, as children of one common Father? How is it that you, being white, do not discriminate against us because of race or color?" To how many white Christians could this be said? Not a great many. And yet if these whites professing religion were really, truly Christian, if the same mind that was in Jesus was in them, not one or two or a dozen but the whole Negro race would be able to say it. These whites professing religion would stand apart from the rest of the white people of the country, would stand on a higher plain, would exhibit a nobler spirit, a more Christlike spirit.

It is important, it seems to me, not only in dealing with race prejudice but in dealing with every other evil, that Christian men and women should understand that Christianity is not clay in the hands of the world-spirit to be molded by it but is itself to be the molder of public sentiment and everything else. It isn't the meal but the leaven put into the meal that is to leaven the whole lump. It is salt—not salt that has lost its savor but the salt of the earth that is intended to arrest corruption, to put an end to the forces that mean moral decay, that tend to break down the tissues of spiritual life and to degenerate into festering sores of race prejudice and all the other brood of evils that grow out of it. The mission of the church, of Christian men and women, is to mold, not be molded by encircling influences of evil. To the shame of the millions of white Christians in this land, the brother in black is still a social and religious outcast.

As I look over this land of ours everywhere I see churches, and these churches in full operation, on weekdays and on the Sabbath. There seems to be no end to religious activities of one kind and another—meetings by day and meetings by night, preaching services, prayer meetings, revival meetings, religious conventions, men's gatherings, great missionary meetings for the conversion of the world, for carrying the gospel to the ends of the earth. And yet right here in America, in the midst of all this missionary activity, this religious zeal, this seeming devotion to Jesus Christ, race prejudice stalks on unhindered. Race prejudice flaunts itself everywhere, unrebuked, as if the Kingdom of Jesus Christ had nothing whatever to do with it, as if it were a thing entirely apart from it. The church is anxious to bring the world to Christ, overflowing with enthusiasm for the conversion of the heathen, and yet indifferent to battle this giant evil right here in Christian America!

On the top of the Central Union Mission Building in this city, near Seventh Street and Pennsylvania Avenue, is a great sign. It consists of a star, and under the star in large letters are the words, "Jesus the light of the world." It is illuminated by electricity and night after night flashes out its message to passers-by. It may be all right to put up such signs, but that is not the way to teach men that Jesus is the Light of the World. The way to do it is not through colored electric lights but through life—by living the religion that we profess, by showing in our daily walk that He is our light, that we are walking in the light, are being transformed through His influence into likeness to Him. Thousands of such electric signs scattered everywhere, piled up to heaven, are not worth as much as one life that is being saved by Christ, commending Him to a sinful world.

And so if our white Christian brethren would give a little less attention to the type of Christianity represented by these religious electric displays, the type of Christianity that is concerned about putting up such signs but is not concerned about this ulcer of race prejudice that is eating out the very vitals of the church; if they would give a little less attention to the evils that are away off and address themselves a little more to some of the evils that are near them; if they would shake off their indifference and show a little interest, just a little, in having the Kingdom of God come into their own hearts and the hearts of their race-hating brethren at home, we would have a little more confidence in their sincerity, and the outlook for the real coming of the Kingdom of God in this land would not be so discouraging.

> *To what purpose is the multitude of your sacrifices unto me? saith the* LORD: *I am full of the burnt offerings of rams, and the fat of fed beasts; and I delight not in the blood of bullocks, or of lambs, or of he goats. When ye come to appear before me, who hath required this at your hand, to tread my courts? Bring no more vain oblations; incense is an abomination unto me; the new moons and sabbaths, the calling of assemblies, I cannot away with; it is iniquity, even the solemn meeting. Your new moons and your appointed feasts my soul hateth: they are a trouble unto me; I am weary to bear them. And when ye spread forth your hands, I will hide mine eyes from you: yea, when ye make many prayers, I will not hear: your hands are full of blood. Wash you, make you clean; put away the evil of your doings from before mine eyes; cease to do evil; Learn to do well; seek judgment, relieve the oppressed, judge the fatherless, plead for the widow*
>
> —ISA. 1:11-17

This is God's message to white Christian America today, I believe, on this matter of race prejudice. Let us hope that it will heed the message and bring forth fruits meet for repentance. A change in the present attitude of the church would be to the interest of both races, would lay the basis for a truer Christian civilization in this land, and would free it from the just imputation that now rests upon it as an abettor and an encourager of race prejudice.

The Religious Aspect of Reconstruction (February 19, 1919)

Dr. Grimké delivered this address at the second annual Convocation for Pastors and Christian Workers sponsored by the School of Theology at Howard University. The address is not about that period following the Civil War known as Reconstruction but about a hoped-for reconstruction or recovery efforts following World War I.

I was asked some weeks ago by Dr. Pratt to take some part in this Convocation and to speak particularly on the religious aspect of reconstruction following this terrible war. The implication in the word *reconstruction* is that there is a need for some new understanding in religious matters as we face the future, as we address ourselves to conditions induced by the war.

I was not quite sure, at the time I was asked to speak, that I understood exactly what was desired of me; nor am I quite sure that I understand now. However, I have jotted down a few thoughts that may answer the purpose or that may be suggestive at least. The question to which I am going to address myself is this: How is the church to meet the religious needs of the men returning from the camps across the water as well as the religious needs of men in general?

In opening this discussion, I observe: (1) The great function of the Christian church is to minister to the spiritual needs of men. It may have other functions, but this is its supreme function. Its paramount obligation lies here. It is the one force or institution in the world, set up by God Himself with a definite spiritual mission—to wit, to bring men back to God, back to divine ideals and standards of living, back to holiness of heart and life. We have foisted so many other things upon it that we are in danger of overlooking, of allowing to sink into the background, the thing for which, more than any other, it ought to stand. This is one secret of its weakness, one reason why it is doing comparatively so little along spiritual lines. It is giving too much of its time to things of minor or secondary importance; it is putting the emphasis in the wrong place. We cannot too strongly impress ourselves with the fact that the function

154

of the church is to meet the spiritual needs of men and that its energies, its resources, should be mainly directed to that end. Whatever else it may succeed in doing, if it fails here, it fails in that which is most vital, in that which is of greatest importance, to the individual as well as to the associated life of man. Only as the church succeeds in bringing men to God, and thus closer to each other, in begetting in them a spirit of brotherhood, of true brotherhood—not a narrow, contracted, racial brotherhood, but a brotherhood of all men—is it functioning properly, realizing the purpose for which it exists, for which it was designed. In Christ Jesus there cannot be Greek or Jew, barbarian, Scythian, bond or free.

(2) The spiritual needs of men, of all men, are fundamentally the same. It doesn't make any difference whether they are white, black, brown, red, or yellow. It doesn't make any difference whether they are rich or poor, high or low, educated or uneducated. It doesn't make any difference whether they are clad in khaki or in civilian's dress, whether they were abroad under the Stars and Stripes or whether they remained at home—they are all human beings; they are all sinners on their way to eternity and judgment. The human heart is the same everywhere, and it is the same today as it was centuries ago, as it was in the days of the apostles, as it was long before their day, as it was in the days of Noah, even reaching back to the days of Adam. What Jeremiah said of it is still true: "The heart is deceitful above all things, and desperately wicked; who can know it?" (Jer. 17:9). What Jesus said of it is still true: "Out of the heart of men, proceed evil thoughts, adulteries, fornications, murders, thefts, covetousness, wickedness, deceit, lasciviousness, an evil eye, blasphemy, pride, foolishness" (Mark 7:21-22). The picture that the apostle Paul draws of the world in the midst of which he was living also gives us a true insight into the character of the human heart:

> And even as they did not like to retain God in their knowledge, God gave them over to a reprobate mind, to do those things which are not convenient; being filled with all unrighteousness, fornication, covetousness, maliciousness; full of envy, murder, strife, debate, malignity; whisperers, backbiters, haters of God, despiteful, proud, boasters, inventors of evil things, disobedient to parents, without understanding, covenant-breakers, without natural affection, implacable, unmerciful.
>
> —ROM. 1:28-31

I do not mean to say, of course, that corrupt human nature reveals itself in all of us in all of these ways. But what I do mean to say is that the possibilities, the latent germs of all of these hateful things, are in the soul of man and may come forth at any time. And it doesn't make any difference how much education he has, how much culture he may possess, what his material circumstances may be, the germs are there just the same. Along with the highest culture may coexist the worst forms of evil. In the palaces as well as in the slums of the city may be found the most debased moral conditions. Education, culture, material well-being leave the human heart essentially the same. The one thing that runs through all humanity is this tendency to evil, this disposition to break away from proper restraints, from the path of rectitude. This is what is meant when, in scriptural language, it is said, "All the world [is] guilty before God" [Rom. 3:19]. "There is none righteous, no, not one. . . . They are all gone out of the way, they are together become unprofitable" (Rom. 3:10-12).

The great outstanding fact that confronts us everywhere is this fact of sin. And in the light of it we have revealed to us what is the great spiritual need of man—it is to get rid of sin; it is to get out from under its guilt and power and into fellowship with God. That is man's greatest need, in comparison with which all other needs are as nothing.

It is in meeting this need that the Christian church comes into prominence and finds its mission, its supreme mission. The task committed to it is the most stupendous that was ever entrusted to any organization. If the church attends to its divinely appointed mission, it will have all that it can possibly do without bothering itself about other things.

This should also be borne in mind in this discussion: The only thing that makes the church of any possible value in dealing with the spiritual needs of man as a sinner is that it has the remedy, the only effectual remedy, for sin, put into its possession by God Himself. And so in addressing itself to this urgent, pressing need of humanity, it may do so with perfect confidence in the efficacy of the remedy. Paul said, "I am not ashamed of the gospel of Christ: for it is the power of God unto salvation to every one that believeth" (Rom. 1:16). And he is speaking here from experience. We have also the words of Peter:

For we have not followed cunningly devised fables, when we made known unto you the power and coming of our Lord Jesus Christ, but were eyewitnesses of his majesty. For he received from God the Father honour and glory, when there came such a voice to him from the excellent glory, This is my beloved Son, in whom I am well pleased. And this voice which came from heaven we heard, when we were with him in the holy mount. We have also a more sure word of prophecy; whereunto ye do well that ye take heed, as unto a light that shineth in a dark place, until the day dawn, and the day star arise in your hearts.

—2 PETER 1:16-19

With these two outstanding facts before us—the fact of man's need, as a sinner, of deliverance from the guilt and power of sin, and the fact that the church has the remedy and the knowledge of the means whereby he may find deliverance—the question for the church to consider, not only now, as a matter of reconstruction, in view of conditions induced by the war, but to be considered at all times, is: What can it do to bring men to repentance and faith and to build them up in holiness of heart and life? What can it do to save sinners, to turn them from darkness to light and from sin and Satan to God and holiness? That is the question that concerns it. Fortunately, in seeking to answer that question we are not left to human wisdom, to the devices of men. God Himself has answered the question for us. God Himself has clearly set forth in His Word how the thing is to be done. We can't improve on His method; and if the church is wise, it will not only seek to find out what has been written for its instruction but will follow it closely, letting everything else go.

To the question, what can the church do to save a lost world, to bring men to repentance and faith in Jesus Christ not only here but everywhere, not only now but at all times, I answer:

1. It can preach the gospel—the gospel of the grace of God in Jesus Christ. This is what Jesus Himself directed His disciples to do. "Go ye into all the world and preach the gospel unto every creature" is what He said to them before He bade them farewell and passed into the skies. He evidently attached very great importance to the preaching of the gospel as a soul-saving agency. It was in that way, through that agency, that He expected to revolutionize the world, to draw men out of it into His Kingdom. And in obedience to His command, this is what the apostles did, what the early disciples did. Wherever they went, they told the good

news, told how God so loved the world that He gave His only begotten Son, that "whosoever believeth in him should not perish, but have everlasting life." And that had its effect; it caught the attention of men. It proved, as the apostle Paul found in his ministry, to be the power of God and the wisdom of God to everyone who believed it.

And this is what the church can do today. This what it must do if it is to minister to the spiritual needs of men. And by the gospel is meant the simple story of Jesus and His love. Isaac Watts wrote these lines:

> Not all the blood of beasts
> On Jewish altars slain
> Could give the guilty conscience peace
> Or wash away the stain.
>
> But Christ, the heavenly Lamb,
> Takes all our sins away;
> A sacrifice of nobler name
> And richer blood than they.

That simple story has done more than anything else to change the human heart, to rescue the perishing.

I was reading the Gospel of John the other day and was very forcibly impressed with the passage, "And I, if I be lifted up from the earth, will draw all men unto me" (12:32). After reading it, I began thinking about it. I saw at once that the lifting up here had reference to Jesus' death upon the cross; and I saw also that He attached very great importance to that lifting up, that beyond it He had great expectations. His vision swept out and all over the world; and what was it that He saw? He saw Himself getting into the thoughts of men everywhere. He saw men everywhere turning to Him, everywhere coming His way, yielding themselves to Him. The thing particularly that impressed me was the statement, "if I be lifted up"—"after I have revealed on Calvary the innermost workings of My heart, the depth and strength of My interest in fallen humanity, then it is that I will begin in earnest the conquest of the world." From Calvary, with pierced hands and feet and a spear thrust in His side, He would make His appeal to the world. And He did not believe that appeal would be in vain; He did not believe that men could listen to the wonderful and touching story of His love and be untouched by it. He was confident of its effect. He said, "I will [not 'may' or 'might'] draw all men unto me."

And He was right. He made no mistake, no miscalculation. The history of the church for the last 1,900 years proves the truth of what He here asserts. Wherever that simple story has been told, in all lands, among all peoples, among all classes and conditions, it has arrested attention; it has been followed by conversions. It hasn't accomplished all that it might have accomplished, but that is not because of any lack of power in it—the fault has been ours. It is because we haven't told it as often as we might have or as earnestly or as sympathetically as we ought to have told it.

I was reading the other day an extract from a sermon by Dr. Edgar Dewitt Jones, in which he quotes a passage from Mr. S. D. Gordon's volume entitled *Prayer Changes Things*. I had not read this particular volume of Mr. Gordon, though I have several others of his, and was glad therefore to run across the extract. This is what Dr. Jones says:

> Mr. S. D. Gordon imagines a conversation between Christ and the Angel Gabriel soon after the ascension. Gabriel is asking Jesus what plans He has made to let all the world know that He lived and died and rose again. And the Master is supposed to reply: "I asked Peter and James and John, and some more of them down there, just go and make it the business of their lives to tell the others. And the others are to tell others, and the others yet others, and still others beyond, till the last man in the farthest reaches has heard the story, and has been caught, thrilled and thrilled by the power of it." But Gabriel looks as if he could see difficulty in the Master's plan, and he says: "Yes, Master, but suppose after a while they forget. Suppose John loses his enthusiasm and simply doesn't tell the others. Suppose their successors away down there in the twentieth century get so busy about things, some of them good things—Church things, maybe—suppose they get so busy that they do not tell the others. What then?" And back came that quiet voice of the Lord Jesus. He says: "Gabriel, I haven't made any other plans. I am counting on them."

I have made this quotation for two reasons: (1) Because it calls attention to the importance of telling the story, the old, old story of Jesus and His love; and (2) because it calls attention to the fact that Jesus is depending upon His church to give the message. He has no other plan of getting

Himself known. How important it is, as Christian men and women, that we should deeply impress ourselves with both of these facts.

And this leads me, in this connection, to call attention to another fact of no less importance, also to be kept in mind. It is not enough that the gospel is preached; it must be with the unction from above, with the baptism of the Holy Spirit. We are so apt to forget that the order issued by the Lord Jesus was not only "Go ye into all the world, and preach the gospel unto every creature" [Mark 16:15], but also "Tarry ye in the city of Jerusalem until ye be endowed with power from on high" (Luke 24:49). That power came upon them on the Day of Pentecost. And what was the result? The impartation to them of new life, energy, power. A sense of a quickening influence unfelt before thrilled through them all. Under that power Peter stood up to preach, and as he preached, men were pricked in their hearts and cried out, "Men and brethren, what shall we do [to be saved]?" And Peter told them what was necessary to be done: "Believe on the Lord Jesus Christ, and thou shall be saved" [as Paul put it later, Acts 16:31]. And they were saved. Three thousand souls as the result of that day's work were added to the church. It is wonderful what the early church succeeded in accomplishing as long as it remained under the Pentecostal baptism, as long as the power of the Spirit rested upon it. Every day souls were being added unto it; every day men were being drawn out of the world into the Kingdom of God.

The simple fact is, there is no use whatever in preaching the gospel unless it is under this Pentecostal power—nothing comes of it, nothing follows; there are no results. Much of our preaching is so perfunctory—a mere formality, a mere routine to be gone through. And this is one reason why so little comparatively results from it. The church needs to be awakened to a sense of the pressing and ever-present need of the presence of the Holy Spirit if it is to do any effective work in saving a lost world. "Not by might, nor by power, but by my spirit, saith the LORD of hosts" (Zech. 4:6). Only where the Spirit is present and works in us and with us and through us may we expect results.

My answer, then, first, to the question, what can the church do in meeting the spiritual needs of the world? is: It can preach the gospel—the gospel, mark you, not something else; not our ideas about salvation or somebody else's ideas; not any man-made philosophy of life but the gospel that has been revealed to us from heaven and preached with the unction from on high, in demonstration of the Spirit and of power. That is the divinely appointed means of saving men. And you can't improve on it; no other program is going to save the world.

2. There is still another thing that the church can do and must do if it is to win men to Christ, if it is to bring them nearer to God and so nearer to each other, if it is to lift them to a higher level of thought, feeling, or action. It must not only preach the gospel, however beautifully and eloquently done, but it must live it. It must not only set Jesus Christ before men by word of mouth, but it must somehow take on the character of Jesus Christ. It must live the Christlike life; it must take the principles of Jesus Christ and exemplify them; it must be what it preaches, what it professes to be. Or at least there must be the earnest and honest effort on its part to carry into every phase of life the spirit of Christ.

What do I mean here by the church? I mean Christian men and women all over the world. I mean all professed followers of the Lord Jesus Christ, of whatever denominational connection—all who have started out to follow Jesus Christ really and truly.

And what am I saying about all such? I am saying that if those who are not Christians are ever to be brought into the Kingdom of God, we who are professedly in it will have to be careful as to how we live. We have to make up our minds and keep them made up, to cut ourselves loose from certain things and to lay hold of others. We have to die unto sin and live unto righteousness. We have got to "put off . . . the old man, which is corrupt . . . and . . . put on the new man, which after God is created in righteousness and true holiness" [Eph. 4:22-24]. No one can read the epistles, even casually, without being greatly impressed with the constant emphasis that is laid upon right living on the part of Christians.

The passages that crowd upon me are:

Have no fellowship with the unfruitful works of darkness. (Eph. 5:11)

Come out from among them, and be ye separate, saith the Lord. (2 Cor. 6:17)

Walk circumspectly, not as fools, but as wise. (Eph. 5:15)

Walk worthy of the vocation wherewith ye are called, with all lowliness and meekness, with long-suffering, forbearing one another in love. (Eph. 4:1-2)

Let all bitterness, and wrath, and anger, and clamour, and evil speaking, be put away from you, with all malice: And be ye kind one to another, tender-hearted, forgiving one another, even as God for Christ's sake hath forgiven you. (Eph. 4:31-32)

I will that thou affirm constantly, that they which have believed in God might be careful to maintain good works. (Titus 3:8)

If ye be reproached for the name of Christ, happy are ye. . . . But let none of you suffer as a murderer, or as a thief, or as an evildoer, or as a busybody in other men's matters. Yet if any man suffer as a Christian, let him not be ashamed. (1 Peter 4:14-16)

Why this constant, incessant emphasis upon right living? For two reasons: (1) Because it is the only kind of life that a Christian ought to live; it is the only kind of life that he can live and be consistent with his profession. (2) Because how he lives will be sure to affect favorably or unfavorably the growth of the Kingdom of Jesus Christ on the earth. It is a fact worth remembering that people judge the value of our religion not by what we say of it, but by what it is actually making of us—by its effect upon our character and life. If it isn't making us better, improving our character, lifting us to higher levels, people will judge it accordingly. It will become a power, as seen in its effects upon us, either to attract or repel.

Last year I read a little volume, *The Jesus of History* by T. R. Glover of St. John's College, Cambridge, England—a very wonderful little book, it seems to me. In the chapter on "The Christian Church in the Roman Empire," after setting forth the condition of the Roman world morally and religiously, a condition that was very, very dark, he describes the coming of the Christian church into the midst of that darkness and the changes that it wrought. The thing particularly that impressed me was the emphasis that he laid upon the character of the men and women of the Christian church in bringing about that change. He accounts for the triumph of the church in these words: "The Christian out-lived the pagan, out-died him, and out-thought him. He came into the world and

lived a great deal better than the pagan; he beat him hollow in living."
Continuing, he says:

> The old world had had morals—plenty of morals—the Stoics over-
> flowed with morals. But the Christian came into the world, not with
> a system of morality—he had rules, indeed. "Which," asks Tertullian,
> "is the ampler rule, Thou shalt not commit adultery, or the rule that
> forbids a single lustful look?" But it was not rules so much that he
> brought into the world as a great passion. "The Son of God," he said,
> "loved me and gave Himself for me. Jesus Christ loved him and gave
> Himself for him. He is the friend of my best Friend. My best Friend
> loves that man, gave Himself for him, died for him." How it alters all the
> relations of life! Who can kill or rob another man, when he remembers
> whose hands were nailed to the cross for that man? See how it bears on
> another side of morality. Tertullian strikes out a great phrase, a new idea
> altogether, when he speaks of "the victim of the common lust." Christ
> died for her—how it safeguards her and uplifts her! Men came into the
> world full of this passion for Jesus Christ. They went to the slave and
> to the temple women and told them: "The Son of God loved you and
> gave Himself for you;" and they believed it and rose into a new life. To
> be redeemed by the Son of God gave the slave a new self-respect, a new
> manhood. He astonished people by His truth, His honesty, His cleanli-
> ness; and there was a new brightness and gayety [sic] about Him. So it
> was with the women. They sang, they overflowed with good temper.
> Of course, there were those who broke down, but Julian the Apostate,
> in his letters to the heathen priests, is a reluctant witness to the higher
> character of the Christian life.

Thus you see, and this is the thing to which I am directing attention,
it was a fact that Christians in their daily living stood upon a higher plain
morally—they lived cleaner, purer lives, which paved the way for the ulti-
mate triumph of Christianity in the Roman Empire. And as it was then,
so it is now, and ever will be. Christianity will triumph just in proportion
as it is represented by men and women who are living on a higher plane
than the world—men and women who reflect the spirit and teachings of
Jesus Christ in their character and in their daily living. Jesus being what
He was, living the kind of life that He lived, no man can represent Him
who is not in sympathy with that kind of life and who is not struggling
to realize it. The representatives of Jesus Christ must be men and women

who have broken with sin, whose minds are made up, fully made up, to do right, to have nothing to do with the unfruitful works of darkness.

The point that I am trying to make here is that the church, as an agency for saving the world, for bringing men to repentance and faith and for building them in holiness of heart and life, must bring to that task, if it hopes to be of any avail, not only an ever-growing sense of the importance of living up to Christian principles but the actual living up to them. If Christian men and women are not going to stand up for what is Christian, are not going to endeavor earnestly and honestly to embody in their actual everyday living the principles of Christianity, of what possible value can they be in advertising and commending it. The only Christianity that is going to have any power over the world, any power to change it, to set it going in the opposite direction from which it is going, is the Christianity that shows, in the character of the men and women who profess it, that it is actually capable of turning out a higher product than is to be found in the world. "Let your light so shine before men, that they may see your good works, and glorify your Father which is in heaven" (Matt. 5:16) is what Jesus said. And in proportion, as the church realizes the importance of doing this, its value as an agency for ministering to the spiritual needs of men will be enhanced.

It is much easier, I know, to preach Christianity than to live it; but whether hard or easy it must be done, for preaching it without living it is of very little value. And one reason why there is widespread indisposition to live it is because the moment we begin in earnest to put on Christ, to grow up into the measure of the stature of His fullness, we find ourselves coming into collision with many things that we are not quite ready to renounce or to take up arms against. And so we disgrace our profession by rendering a kind of lukewarm, halfhearted service, by pursuing a kind of good Lord, good devil policy, not altogether for God, and not altogether for the devil, trying to make terms with both, and always ending by doing the bidding of the devil.

The trouble with the Christian church today is:

1. It lacks conviction, moral conviction. It doesn't seem to be able to make up its mind as to what is right and what is wrong. It seems to accept the Bible as the rule of faith and practice but doesn't seem to know exactly where it stands on a great many things. And these doubts always spring up in dealing with practical difficulties, with things that run

counter to popular sentiment. How long it takes to get it to take a stand on popular evils, to express itself. Take the matter of race prejudice, an evil that curses the whole world and this country in particular as scarcely anything else does, an evil that is rampant everywhere in this land, and out of which the most dreadful things have come and are still coming. Is race prejudice right or wrong, Christian or anti-Christian? Is it in harmony with the spirit and teaching of Jesus Christ or not? The church seems to have no conviction on the subject. It doesn't seem to know; it hasn't yet made up its mind. No one believes, of course, that it doesn't know; it simply doesn't suit its convenience to know. The ignorance that it professes is only feigned; it doesn't really exist.

2. The church not only lacks moral conviction, in the sense that it often doesn't seem to know where it stands, but even where it knows, its convictions often are not deep-rooted. They don't seem to take a very firm hold upon it, to sink their roots deep down into the subsoil of the soul. The church doesn't seem to possess the spirit of what Carlyle calls "the Everlasting Yea and the Everlasting Nay"—convictions of right and wrong that root themselves in the deepest fibers of the soul, convictions by which men live and for which they are ready to die. It has convictions but holds them very lightly; it has convictions but is very little influenced by them—what James calls a dead faith.

3. The church lacks courage—the willingness to face danger, to suffer, and even to die rather than swerve from what it believes to be right, the spirit that says always and everywhere, "We must obey God rather than man." It is lack of this spirit that is one of the serious obstacles in the way of combating certain evils in the world today. It is the great obstacle in the way of combating race prejudice. I cannot believe that the men who occupy the pulpits of this land, assuming that they are men of ordinary intelligence and common sense and that they have, as they ought to have as leaders, some little knowledge, at least, of the Word of God, are without some convictions on the subject, that they do not know that it is wrong, contrary to every principle of Christianity. And yet it is almost impossible to get a syllable from them on the subject, except here and there occasionally. Why? Simply because it is an unpopular subject; because the men and women to whom they speak Sabbath after Sabbath, and upon whom they are dependent for their bread and butter, are full of prejudice and would resent any attempt on their part to set them right.

This is what they are afraid of. They are not willing to run the risk of offending those upon whom they are dependent; they are not willing to run the risk of jeopardizing their personal interest, their material well-being. And so they say nothing; they pass it over in silence, and thus the evil grows and will continue to grow until God raises up a ministry with enough courage and backbone to smite it as it ought to be smitten.

I confess, I have always had a kind of contempt for the spirit that in the face of wrong hesitates to speak out for fear of giving offense, of losing caste, of suffering in the good opinion of evildoers, the perpetrators of wrong.

> *Truth forever on the scaffold,*
> *Wrong forever on the throne,—*
> *Yet that scaffold sways the future,*
> *And, behind the dim unknown,*
> *Standeth God within the shadow,*
> *Keeping watch above his own.*

So wrote James Russell Lowell.

The man who is not willing to go to the scaffold with truth, to suffer for the sake of truth, who hasn't enough faith in God to go forward in the path of right and of duty regardless of personal consequences, is unfit to represent Jesus Christ and has no function that he can properly perform in helping in the Kingdom of God, in meeting the spiritual needs of the world. Men of that stamp are nothing but hirelings. What are hirelings but men who are afraid to speak out for fear of offending those upon whom they are dependent for their bread and butter.

The church that is to win the world to Christ is the church that lifts up the standard that God has set up whether the world approves or not. It takes courage to be a Christian; it takes courage to follow Jesus Christ. One of the most wonderful things to me in the early days of Christianity was the courage displayed by those early Christians—how in obedience to Jesus Christ they went forth into the midst of a hostile world, with public sentiment and everything against them; how in the face of danger, privation, suffering, and death, they held on uncompromisingly to Christian principles. They were willing to suffer, willing to be killed for them, but they were not willing to surrender them. So many of them suffered; many of them were martyred. And thus victory finally came.

How different is the spirit of the church today. It is willing to follow Christ, to stand up for Christian principles, only so far as it suits its own purpose to do so, only so far as it entails no hardships, only so far as it accords with popular sentiment. Dr. Arthur Cushman McGiffert, in his article "Christianity and Democracy" in the January 1919 issue of the *Harvard Theological Review*, speaking of the church, says—and I am quoting his words because they confirm what I am saying here: "Christian opinion usually follows the prevailing opinion of the world at large. Seldom, to its shame be it said, has the Church ventured upon new paths until common sentiment has pronounced them safe." And what he says is true. Timidity, cowardice, is one of the church's most conspicuous characteristics.

I have spoken quite long enough. Let me now sum up what I have been trying to say.

The great function of the church is to minister to the spiritual needs of men.

The spiritual needs of men are fundamentally the same all over the world, regardless of race or condition; all men are sinners on their way to eternity and judgment. The taint of sin runs through all. These needs are to be met:

(1) By the faithful preaching of the gospel, the pure, unadulterated gospel, the gospel of the love of God as revealed in Jesus Christ, preached under the Spirit's influence, the baptism from on high. (2) These needs are to be met by living the gospel, by exemplifying in our character and lives the principles of the religion that we profess, by letting our light shine, by growing up into the measure of the stature of the fullness of Christ.

If the church is to do the work that is entrusted to it:

1. It must not lose sight of its great mission as a spiritual force. It must not be dabbling in too many things. Paul said, "I am determined not to know any thing among you, save Jesus Christ, and him crucified" (1 Cor. 2:2).

2. It must have convictions, moral convictions. It must know right from wrong. It must know what it stands for.

3. These convictions must be something more than mere passing whims or caprices; they must be abiding certainties, or to borrow the language of one of our poets [James Russell Lowell]:

. . . the fiery pith,
The compact nucleus, round which systems grow;
Mass after mass becomes inspired therewith,
And whirls impregnate with the central glow.

4. It must have the courage of its convictions. It must dare to assert what it believes and dare to live what it asserts.

5. It must feel, and feel deeply, the importance, the transcendent importance, of its mission and must address itself earnestly to it. The apostle says, "Necessity is laid upon me; yea, woe is unto me, if I preach not the gospel" (1 Cor. 9:16). And again: "As much as in me is, I am ready to preach the gospel to you that are at Rome also" (Rom. 1:15). The utmost is what he wanted to do; and that is the spirit in which the church must carry on its work.

6. It must also do all that it does or attempts to do in dependence upon God, in the consciousness of the fact that its sufficiency is not in itself but in God. Only as it works in dependence upon God can it hope to do any effective work.

The longer I live, the more I am impressed with the fact that what we Christians need is greater earnestness, the spirit of entire consecration, such a sense of the value of spiritual things that we will be willing to let everything else go in order to possess them. The merchantman who found the pearl of great price went and sold all that he had and bought it. And that is the estimate that we Christians must put upon the things of God, upon this wonderful, divine life that we have started out to live, if through us the world is to be won to Christ.

Nothing is more apparent, on the face of things, than the utter shallowness of much of our profession, the utter lack of sincerity. We profess to accept Jesus Christ; we profess to accept His standard of values. And what that standard is we have in His own glorious character and life and in the Word of God, in the Scriptures of the Old and the New Testaments.

What evidence do we give that we are honest, that we are sincere, that we mean from the bottom of our hearts just what we say and just what such a profession implies? Alas, the words of Jesus are as applicable today as when He uttered them: "Why call ye me, Lord, Lord, and do not the things which I say?" (Luke 6:46). The church must face that question; we Christian men and women must face it and give an honest answer to it if we are to be fit instruments to do the Lord's work. We can't hope to impress the world with our sincerity, with our honesty, when in so many, many ways we deny the authority of Jesus. We do not do what He commands us to do but what we choose to do, regardless of His wishes. The church that is to be the instrument in the hand of God for bringing the world to Christ must not only profess to believe in Jesus Christ as prophet, priest, and king. It must be actually sitting at His feet and learning from Him. It must be actually relying upon His blood for cleansing, and relying upon it with such an apprehension of the heinousness of sin as to hate it, to turn away from it. It must be actually obeying Jesus Christ, doing the things that He wants it to do, going the way that He wants it to go.

A body of men and women bound together around Jesus Christ as leader, with the great ideals of His religion clearly apprehended and with the earnest purpose, the steady, persistent, never-ending effort to realize those ideals in the midst of a sinful world and unconformed to it, would cause that world to stop and take notice as nothing else would.

God is calling the church today, as never before, to come out from the world, to have nothing to do with the unfruitful works of darkness, to rise and shine. "Awake, awake; put on thy strength, O Zion; put on thy beautiful garments, O Jerusalem, the holy city: for henceforth there shall no more come into thee the uncircumcised and the unclean. Shake thyself from the dust; loose thyself from the bands of thy neck" [Isa. 52:1-2]. May God hasten the time when the church shall hear that call and rise to the full measure of its great opportunities in ministering to the spiritual needs of the world.

As a minister of Jesus Christ in this so-called work of spiritual reconstruction, I have nothing new to offer, nothing better to offer than I have been offering for the last forty years—the gospel of the grace of God in Christ Jesus; the taking of Christ's yoke upon us and learning of Him; denying ourselves and taking up our cross daily and following Him through evil report as well as good. Others may have something new, something better to offer, but I have not, and I have no disposition to seek for anything else or any desire to offer anything else. So far as the world has been saved, the gospel preached and lived is the only thing that has saved it, and the only thing that will continue to save it.

All this talk about reconstruction, to my mind, is scarcely more than a passing fad, a mere effervescence on the surface, an effort to seem to be doing something new. Only as the old, old story of the cross is relied upon and presented with ever-increasing clearness and power will men be saved. No newfangled notions or methods will amount to anything. When this work of spiritual reconstruction is over, it will reduce itself ultimately to the old way of teaching and inspiring men along the lines set forth in the Word of God, with Jesus Christ and His ideals as the great objective.

"Whoever," said Jesus, "heareth these words of mine, and doeth them, I will liken him unto a wise man, which built his house upon a rock: And the rain descended, and the floods came, and the winds blew, and beat upon that house; and it fell not: for it was founded upon a rock" (Matt. 7:24-25).

Work built upon that foundation needs no reconstruction.

Christ's Program for the Saving of the World (February 28, 1936)

Author's note: This sermon is published because I believe it deals with a matter that is of vital importance to the progress of the Kingdom of God. It is hoped that it will be carefully read by young ministers, especially, and by those who are preparing for the ministry in our theological seminaries.

> *And Jesus came and spake unto them, saying, All power is given unto me in heaven and in earth. Go ye therefore, and teach all nations, baptizing them in the name of the Father, and of the Son, and of the Holy Ghost: teaching them to observe all things whatsoever I have commanded you: and, lo, I am with you always, even unto the end of the world.*
>
> — MATTHEW 28:18-20

> *And he said unto them, Go ye into all the world, and preach the gospel to every creature.*
>
> — MARK 16:15

These are the words of Jesus after He had laid down His precious life on the cross and had risen triumphant from the grave, uttered just before His ascension.

With a full knowledge of conditions, even at their worst, in the words I have read as my text He outlined His program for salvation, for accomplishing the great task for which He had come and for which His Kingdom was set up on the earth. It was to redeem the world, to set things right, to bring about changes for the better in all the relations of life.

Bear in mind also that at that time the world was passing through what perhaps was its darkest period morally. Everywhere things were on the downward grade. Society in all its branches was rotten to the core, steeped in iniquities of every kind.

And yet Jesus, the great Optimist, believed it could be redeemed and committed the execution of His plan for its redemption to His followers, to the men who believed in Him, who had accepted Him as the Messiah,

171

and who had associated themselves with Him to carry on the glorious undertaking after He was gone.

Let us see now what His program is for redeeming a lost world, for bringing about changes for the better.

(1) He says, "Go." Go and do what? Go and preach the gospel. What is the gospel? What is He referring to particularly? What is it that they were to preach? The great fact set forth in John 3:16: "For God so loved the world, that he gave his only begotten Son, that whosoever believeth in him should not perish, but have everlasting life."

It is the astounding fact that God, the Creator of heaven and earth, was so interested in rescuing men from the power of sin and Satan that He willingly gave His only begotten Son, His well-beloved Son, to die in order to open a way of escape for the sinner from the guilt and power of sin. Hence the statement, "Ye were not redeemed with corruptible things, as silver and gold . . . but with the precious blood of Christ" [1 Pet. 1:18-19].

This gospel message carries with it certain things that must be kept ever to the front:

For one, the fact of sin and its deadly nature. The disposition now, in a large measure, is to do away with the idea of sin, to do away with it altogether, or to minimize it, explain it away, or attach little or no importance to it. But the gospel conception of sin and its attitude toward it is very different. Sin not only exists but is most deadly in character and if not arrested will inevitably lead to death—physical death, moral death, spiritual death.

One of the things that Jesus lays down as fundamental in His scheme of redemption is that men must realize that they are sinners, that they are not living as they ought to live—a God-centered instead of a self-centered life.

The fact of sin in Christ's scheme of redemption is fundamental and must be kept to the front. Men must not be allowed to forget the fact that they are sinners and that the wages of sin is death.

This is a doctrine that men don't like to hear about. They know that they are sinners, but they try to forget it. This is why often they plunge into all kinds of frivolities in order to get away from the serious thought of sin and its fatal consequences. This is why, unfortunately, in order to comply with or not to offend that kind of sentiment, many pulpits have little or nothing to say about sin.

One thing we may be sure of: as this aspect of man's condition drops out of our preaching, things will steadily grow worse, and men will become more and more set in their evil ways. For if there is no such thing as sin, or no evil consequences to follow, then there is no reason why we shouldn't open all the floodgates of passions and evil inclinations and desires and let things go at full speed, no reason why we should not adopt as our philosophy of life the motto, "Let us eat and drink, for tomorrow we die." It is to save men from that stupid, foolish delusion that Christ makes imperative in His plan of rescue the necessity of stressing, and stressing with ever-increasing emphasis, the fact of sin as man's most serious problem.

The other thing that is included in the gospel message is the publication of God's plan for the saving of sinners—namely, repentance and faith in Jesus Christ. In Romans 8:3-4 we read, "For what the law could not do, in that it was weak through the flesh, God sending his own Son in the likeness of sinful flesh, and for sin, condemned sin in the flesh: that the righteousness of the law might be fulfilled in us, who walk not after the flesh, but after the Spirit."

Jesus says it is the spreading of the knowledge of this great and glorious fact that must go on as a part of His plan for the saving of the world, for bettering conditions.

This is what the apostle Paul had in mind in his first epistle to the Corinthians where he says:

> For Christ sent me not to baptize, but to preach the gospel: not with wisdom of words, lest the cross of Christ should be made of none effect. For the preaching of the gospel is to them that perish foolishness; but unto us who are saved it is the power of God. For it is written, I will destroy the wisdom of the wise, and will bring to nothing the understanding of the prudent. Where is the wise? where is the scribe? where is the disputer of this world? hath not God made foolish the wisdom of this world? For after that in the wisdom of God the world by wisdom knew not God, it pleased God by the foolishness of preaching to save them that believe. For the Jews require a sign, and the Greeks seek after wisdom: But we preach Christ crucified, unto the Jews a stumbling block, and unto the Greeks foolishness; but unto them which are called, both Jews and Greeks, Christ the power of God, and the wisdom of God.

—1:17-24

There are still some who feel that this way of saving the world is foolishness. They have other schemes to suggest that they think are better.

(2) Notice now what is the next element in His program for saving the world, for bettering conditions. It is contained in the words, "Go ye therefore, and teach all nations . . . teaching them to observe all things whatsoever I have commanded you." It is evident that the change that He wishes to effect for the better is to be brought about in part by teaching. His plan takes both preaching and teaching.

And here we are directed not only to teach but what we are to teach. It is not secular knowledge that He is here particularly concerned about, important as that kind of knowledge may be. The knowledge He has in mind is that which is contained in the Old Testament Scriptures, which He had endorsed as the Word of God, supplemented by what He had added of His own and what was still to be added through inspired men, all embodied in what is now known as the Bible, the Word of God, embracing both Testaments.

In this campaign for saving a lost world, for bettering conditions, the contents of this Book must be carefully studied and taught, line upon line, precept upon precept, here a little and there a little, in season and out of season. Thus we should understand and see that careful provision is made, under competent teachers, for the study of the Word of God.

The importance of teaching the Word of God as a part of the regular program of saving men, of improving conditions around us, will be manifest to anyone who stops and thinks for a moment. The object of this teaching is to familiarize men with the contents of the Scriptures of the Old and New Testaments.

What a book the Bible is! Where in all the world's literature will you find such a storehouse of knowledge and wisdom? Where will you find such sublime ideas about God, such noble standards of living? Open it anywhere, and how the light flashes in upon us as from no other source. Take the Ten Commandments, the Sermon on the Mount, the thirteenth chapter of 1 Corinthians, the warnings and exhortations found in the Gospels and epistles, and above all the glorious character and life of Jesus Christ.

What greater influence could be brought to bear upon the uplift of humanity, upon changing things for the better, than a knowledge of the contents of this Book widely diffused? This seems to be foreshadowed by what the prophet Isaiah says in 11:9: "They shall not hurt nor destroy in all my holy mountain: for the earth shall be full of the knowledge of the LORD, as the waters cover the sea." With the diffusion of the knowledge of God through the circulation of this Book of God, wonderful things are promised. And wonderful changes for the better do actually occur when God's Word is carefully taught among the people.

In an address recently delivered by Dr. John R. Mott in connection with the American Bible Society's celebration of the one hundredth anniversary of its labors in China, these words occur:

> De Quincey said that all literature is divided into the literature of knowledge and the literature of power. The Bible constitutes preeminently the literature of power. I am not a mystic. I wish I were more so. I certainly am not suspicious; but how often I have observed that this literature, when intelligently studied, expounded, and applied, seems to vibrate with power not of this world! You ask, What kind of power? Well, power to shake conscience; to make conscience afraid, perchance, at times, to create conscience.
>
> On my trip down in South America I put the question to a group of students, "What is the greatest obstacle to Christianity?" One of them quickly replied, "The Ten Commandments," by which he meant that the Commandments, expounded and applied, shake conscience, create conviction of sin, and necessitate radical changes. Moreover, they help to keep conscience sensitive and responsive. In fact, I find that when I am where there is the greatest responsiveness to duty and high idealism I am where there has been the most faithful application as well as interpretation and acceptance of these sacred writings.
>
> The Bible has power to energize the will. In one of my student evangelistic campaigns in Australia a Jewish student made this striking remark to me after one of my addresses: "These writings not only hold up high ideals to me, and afford teachings that my reason accepts, but they also make me want to obey them." That is, they communicate divine impulses as well as persuasion of mind, moving of the heart, and kindling of the imagination; yes, power to energize the will from palsy into high efficiency.

And yet how often we find men in our pulpits searching heaven and earth for something new to preach about, while this treasure-house of wisdom and knowledge, of the things necessary to salvation, is neglected, passed by, and overlooked.

175

Dr. Alexander MacLaren, the great Bible student and expositor, was once asked the best way to study the Bible. Clenching his fist and bringing it down on the table, he said, "Dig, dig, dig, dig down into its meaning." "Yes," said the inquirer, "but what then, Doctor?" He replied, "Dig, dig, dig again." But that is just what so many of us are not willing to do and why we wander off into so many strange fields in search of materials for our pulpit ministrations.

(3) Another element in this redemptive program of Jesus is: this preaching and teaching are to be carried into all the world and to all nations. His aim is to carry the blessings of salvation to the whole human race. The great missionary fields lying beyond us must also claim our attention in working out this great plan of redemption. To be interested in home missions is not enough; we must think of those on the foreign field as well. The command is, "Go ye into all the world." And only as our sympathy goes out to all are we exhibiting His spirit or obeying His command.

(4) The fourth thing to which attention is directed in this redemptive program of Jesus is contained in the words, "And, lo, I am with you always, even unto the end of the world." Jesus had committed to His apostles a tremendous task, a task involving great responsibilities, dangers, and hardships. These men had been accustomed to His leadership, to looking to Him for everything; now He is going to leave them, to be no longer visibly among them—what will they do without Him in the hour of need, when troubles come, when dangers assail them, when they are confronted on all sides by bitter and relentless enemies?

He tells them, "Don't be afraid. Though no longer visible, I will still be with you." And you will notice, He not only says, "I am [will be] with you," but "always"—i.e., at all times and under all circumstances. And even more, He goes on to say to them that He would be with them "unto the end of the world." "There will be no time when I will not be with you." To the eye of sense He would be away, but to the eye of faith He would be still among them and still available for every need.

The appeal was clearly to their faith. They knew Him; they knew He could be trusted, that His word could be relied upon. And with His word to rely upon, they went forth confident that He would be with them. And He *was* with them. And it was by His being with them and working with them and through them that mighty things were done, that mighty works were accomplished.

(5) One thing more is contained in these words that we are considering, outlining His program for saving the world, for bettering conditions. It is contained in the very first part of the great announcement: "And Jesus came and spake unto them, saying, All power is given unto me in heaven and in earth."

That is an amazing statement for anyone to make, but Jesus made it. And from what we know of His character, He never would have made it had it not been true. And the more we think of it, the more astounding does it seem. It is not, mark you, *some* power in heaven and in earth, but *all* power in heaven and in earth.

I am calling attention to this stupendous accession of power on the part of Jesus as a guarantee to us of all needed help in the prosecution of this work of redeeming the world. All power is committed unto Him. Nothing lies beyond His reach. His resources are adequate for every need. No task, therefore, is too great to undertake in His name, no difficulties too hard to be encountered and overcome, and no enemies too formidable to confront. We need have no fear, therefore, in going forth in His name.

No fear—

1. As to support. So many of us, in doing the Lord's work, put the matter of support first and make everything else subservient to our creature comfort, fearing to do anything or say anything that might result in cutting off supplies, forgetful of the fact that God has promised to take care of His workers. All we have to do is to be faithful in doing the work committed to us. If we seek first the Kingdom and His righteousness, the things necessary to creature comforts will be supplied. That is the promise.

2. Nor need we have any fear as to opposition. Paul said, "We wrestle not against flesh and blood, but against principalities, against powers, against the rulers of the darkness of this world, against spiritual wickedness in high places" (Eph. 6:12). He was not afraid, however, to go forth in the strength of the Lord to encounter the enemy. So in all our encounters with the forces of evil in the service of the Lord we may always hear sounding in our ears the assuring words, "Fear not; fear not. Lo, I am with you always."

And now a word more in bringing this discourse to a close. Two things I have had in mind in the preparation and preaching of it:

1. To call attention specifically to Christ's program for saving the world, for bringing about changes for the better in individuals and in communities—in the whole structure of society, in all human relationships.

a. It is by preaching the gospel—the gospel of the grace of God in Christ Jesus.

b. It is by teaching—teaching not philosophy or science or any special department of human knowledge, but teaching what is written in the Scriptures, the Word of God, given by holy men as they were moved by the Holy Spirit. It is making known the contents of the Bible that Jesus here links up with the work of saving the world, of bringing about changes for the better in all human relations and conditions.

2. My purpose in the preparation and preaching of this discourse is to call attention to the fact that though the plan, as here outlined, is perfect, is in every way adapted to accomplish the object for which it was intended, and has been in operation for nearly two thousand years, comparatively little, compared to what might have been done, has been accomplished. There seems to be just as much evil in the world today as there ever was. The devil seems to be just as firmly entrenched in power today as in the days of Christ.

This much may be said, however: while wickedness still goes on, while the broad way that leads to death is still crowded, there are a great many more good people in the world today—people who are really trying to do right, people who have been influenced by the spirit and teachings of Jesus Christ—than when His Kingdom was set up centuries ago. Some changes for the better, and some very remarkable changes, have taken place under its operations.

This world is still wicked—yes, very, very wicked. But there are a great many more people now who can be counted on the side of righteousness than before Jesus sent out His disciples with instructions to go into all the world and preach the gospel to every creature, teaching them to observe all things whatsoever He had commanded them.

Something has been accomplished, though not as much as might have been expected. And I want to stop just a moment to tell you why so little has been accomplished.

It is because those who have been entrusted with carrying out His program have to a very large extent been recreant to the trust committed to them. How many of our ministers have been following faithfully and earnestly the program here laid down by the Master? How faithfully have they been preaching the gospel?

They have preached on almost everything except Jesus Christ as the Lamb of God whose blood alone cleanses from sin. The thought of sin, from which we need to be saved, has largely dropped out of most of our preaching.

How many of our ministers have sought carefully to expound the Word of God, setting forth clearly before the people the teachings of the inspired volume concerning character and conduct, line upon line, precept upon precept, here a little and there a little, in season and out of season?

People attend the churches, but rarely are their consciences pricked. They attend the churches but hear little about their sins and shortcomings. They attend the churches, but their self-complacency is never disturbed by what they hear, or at least rarely. They hear and go away feeling no sense of lack on their part and no wish or desire to live more worthily than they are living. Divine unrest rarely stirs within them; no welling up of great and ennobling desires is awakened within them. The people listen and go away to gossip, to tattle, to keep on in their evil ways.

Louis XIV is reported as having said once to Bossuet, the court preacher, "How is it that when I hear the other great court preachers I go away delighted; but when I hear you I go away greatly dissatisfied with myself?" Alas, alas, too many of our preachers, like the other court preachers, send the people away delighted by dealing in glittering generalities and by keeping as far away as possible from the sins that beset them, the sins of which they are guilty. Under much of the preaching that is heard, nobody goes away greatly dissatisfied with himself or herself. That kind of preaching may bring popularity to the preacher but leanness to the souls of the hearers.

How many of our preachers feed their own souls on the Word of God and always draw their sermons and exhortations from the Word of God? The reason there has not been more progress in saving the world is because we have not been doing what we have been directed to do. We have not been preaching the gospel and teaching the people out of the Word of God as we ought to have been doing. And things will never be any better until we swing in line with the plan as here laid down by Jesus

Christ. Under this plan every evil now afflicting both old and young will be reached, and effectively reached.

Under this plan, therefore, every church ought to be operating. Nothing should be allowed to go on in it or under its direction that does not have one or both of these ends in view—the turning of men from their evil ways and attaching them to Jesus Christ as their Lord and Savior or the bringing of them under the power and influence of some Bible truth. Every meeting should have some such object in view; every sermon, every address or exhortation, should be keyed to the same definite aims and purposes.

When all of our churches and all of our ministers realize what the work is to which they are called and get busy doing it, then, and not until then, will changes for the better take place, will the Kingdom of God come, and come with power. The more we get away from the gospel in our preaching and away from the teaching of the Scriptures in regard to character and conduct, the greater will be the swing away from the things that are true, just, pure, lovely, and of good report.

What we need most of all is a faithful, courageous, consecrated ministry that will stick close to the Word of God in all its ministrations and in dependence upon the Holy Spirit to make effective the Word preached and taught.

Such is Christ's program for saving the world, and it can't be improved on. The world can be saved in no other way.

Dr. Joseph Parker, the great London preacher, laying the cornerstone of a church in London, once said:

> I do not want every man to preach in the same way as I do, but I want every man to preach the same gospel. Believe me, nothing but the gospel will stand the wear and tear of experience and evolution and rivalry.
>
> Ministers of London: Be faithful to your Saviour, and He will be faithful to you! Invent some superficial gospel of your own, and your efforts will end in disappointment and mockery. Preach the gospel of the Son of God, and you will find that it is the power of God unto salvation.

Those are timely words for preachers everywhere, and never more so than today. Christ's program for saving a lost world needs to be revived and pushed with vigor. Everywhere, throughout the whole church, this note for renewed effort to carry out Christ's program for saving the world ought to be sounded, and all the forces gotten in line for its execution. We need to wake up to the fact that

> *We are not here to play, to dream, to drift;*
> *We have hard work to do, and loads to lift.* [Maltbie Babcock]

If we are not going to preach the gospel and teach the Word of God faithfully, we have no business in the ministry. And the sooner we get out of it, the better.

The question is sometimes asked, what is to be the future of Christianity as it comes into competition with other religions and with Communism, Nationalism, Capitalism, and all antagonistic forces? To my mind there is absolutely no need to worry about that matter. Jesus said, after hearing Peter's great confession, "Upon this rock I build my church; and the gates of hell shall not prevail against it" (Matt. 16:18).

In Revelation 6:2 we also read, "And I saw, and behold a white horse: and he that sat on him had a bow; and a crown was given unto him: and he went forth conquering, and to conquer."

In Revelation 1:17-18 we read, "Fear not; I am the first and the last: I am he that liveth, and was dead; and, behold, I am alive for evermore. Amen; and have the keys of hell and death." We read also, "Not by might, nor by power, but by my Spirit, saith the LORD of hosts. Who art thou, O great mountain? Before Zerubbabel thou shalt become a plain" (Zech. 4:6-7). And in Daniel we read, "A stone was cut out without hands, which smote the image . . . [and] became a great mountain, and filled the whole earth" (2:34-35).

The only thing that we need to be concerned about is to see that we carry out faithfully the instructions of our Lord; that we be true to the solemn trust committed to us; that we go on preaching the gospel; that we go on teaching His word, line upon line, precept upon precept, here a little and there a little, in season and out of season, and give ourselves no concern about its future. Its future is assured. God is behind it. It cannot fail.

Let us stop worrying about the future of Christianity and get down to hard work in carrying out the instructions of our Lord.

NOTES

Part I: Lemuel Haynes

1. Timothy Mather Cooley, *Sketches of the Life and Character of the Rev. Lemuel Haynes, A.M., for Many Years Pastor of a Church in Rutland, Vt., and Later in Granville, New York* (1837; reprint, New York: Negro Universities Press, 1969).

2. Helen MacLam, "Introduction: Black Puritan on the Northern Frontier," in Richard Newman, ed., *Black Preacher to White America: The Collected Writings of Lemuel Haynes, 1774–1833* (New York: Carlson, 1990), p. xx.

3. Ibid.

4. John Saillant, *Black Puritan, Black Republican: The Life and Thought of Lemuel Haynes, 1753–1833* (New York: Oxford University Press, 2003), p. 4.

5. MacLam, "Introduction: Black Puritan on the Northern Frontier," in Newman, ed., *Black Preacher to White America: The Collected Writings of Lemuel Haynes, 1774–1833*, p. xxxv.

6. Haynes used 1 Thessalonians 2:19 as his key text for the funeral sermon of the Rev. Abraham Carpenter. The text reads: "For what is our hope, or joy, or crown of rejoicing? Are not even ye in the presence of our Lord Jesus Christ at his coming?"

Part II: Bishop Daniel A. Payne

1. Daniel Alexander Payne, *Recollection of Seventy Years* (Nashville: AME Sunday School Union, 1888), p. 14.

2. Ibid., p. 17.

3. Ibid.

4. Francis J. Grimké, "Addresses Dealing with the Careers of Distinguished Americans: Bishop Daniel Alexander Payne," delivered December 10 and 17, 1893. In Carter G. Woodson, ed., *The Works of Francis J. Grimké, Volume I: Addresses Mainly Personal and Racial* (Washington, DC: The Associated Publishers, Inc., 1942), p. 2.

5. Payne, *Recollection of Seventy Years*, pp. 27-28.

6. Benjamin F. Lee, "The Centenary of Daniel Alexander Payne, Fourth Bishop of the African Methodist Episcopal Church," *Church Review*, 28 (1), July 1911: 423-429.

7. Francis J. Grimké, "Addresses Dealing with the Careers of Distinguished Americans: Bishop Daniel Alexander Payne," p. 8.

8. Payne, *Recollection of Seventy Years*, pp. 109-110.

9. Ibid., p. 137.

10. Ibid., pp. 92, 133, 149.

11. The term *tippling* referred to drinking alcoholic beverages. Payne and many of his contemporaries actively supported temperance and the Temperance Movement. They

saw the ravaging effects of drinking alcohol on the freeborn and emancipated brethren and communities and denounced the social practice as anathema to freedom and advancement.

Part III: Francis J. Grimké

1. Henry J. Ferry, *Francis James Grimké: Portrait of a Black Puritan* (New Haven, CT: Yale University, Ph.D. dissertation, 1970). Ferry's dissertation is the only book-length treatment of the life of Grimké.
2. Ibid., p. 9.
3. Francis J. Grimké, *The Works of Francis J. Grimké, Vol. 3: Stray Thoughts and Meditations* (Washington, DC: Associated Publishers, Inc., 1942).
4. Ibid., pp. 53-56.
5. Carter G. Woodson, Introduction, *The Works of Francis J. Grimké, Vol. 3: Stray Thoughts and Meditations*, p. iv.
6. Francis J. Grimké, "Addresses Dealing with the Careers of Distinguished Americans: Bishop Daniel Alexander Payne," in Carter G. Woodson, ed., *The Works of Francis J. Grimké, Vol. 1: Addresses Mainly Personal and Racial* (Washington, DC: Associated Publishers, Inc., 1942), p. 13.

SCRIPTURE INDEX

GENERAL INDEX